MADAM JUSTICE: AN INSIDE LOOK

Previous Irwin Law Books By This Author

Mediation for Lawyers: A Practical Guide for Effective Representation of Your Clients (2024)

Madam Justice: An Inside Look

Suzanne Handman

UNIVERSITY OF TORONTO PRESS
Toronto Buffalo London

Irwin Law
An imprint of University of Toronto Press
Toronto Buffalo London
utppublishing.com
Printed in Canada

ISBN: 978-1-4875-6946-4 (paper) | ISBN: 978-1-4875-6947-1 (PDF)
ISBN: 978-1-4875-6948-8 (EPUB)

Library and Archives Canada Cataloguing in Publication

Title: Madam justice : an inside look / Suzanne Handman.
Names: Handman, Suzanne, author.
Description: Includes bibliographical references and index.
Identifiers: Canadiana (print) 20250143178 | Canadiana (ebook) 20250143194 | ISBN 9781487569464 (paper) | ISBN 9781487569488 (EPUB) | ISBN 9781487569471 (PDF)
Subjects: LCSH: Handman, Suzanne. | LCSH: Women judges—Canada—Biography. | LCSH: Judges—Canada—Biography. | LCSH: Judgments—Canada. | LCSH: Court proceedings—Canada. | LCGFT: Autobiographies.
Classification: LCC KE416.H36 A3 2025 | DDC 347/.014092—dc23

Cover design: Mary Beth MacLean
Cover image: Mr. Soufiane Zaari

We wish to acknowledge the land on which the University of Toronto Press operates. This land is the traditional territory of the Wendat, the Anishnaabeg, the Haudenosaunee, the Métis, and the Mississaugas of the Credit First Nation.

University of Toronto Press acknowledges the financial support of the Government of Canada, the Canada Council for the Arts, and the Ontario Arts Council, an agency of the Government of Ontario, for its publishing activities.

Canada Council for the Arts
Conseil des Arts du Canada

Funded by the Government of Canada
Financé par le gouvernement du Canada
Canada

To my husband Bjørn U. Ellingsen
My very best friend and partner for life

Summary Table of Contents

Detailed Table of Contents

Acknowledgements

I wish to thank all my friends, colleagues, and family who provided me with their comments and suggestions for my book. First and foremost, I thank my husband, Bjørn U. Ellingsen, without whose help I would not have written this book. He not only read and commented on my first draft, giving me invaluable advice and support, but he also helped me navigate the technical challenges of word processing on my PC.

I rewrote my text after it languished on my computer for many months. This rewritten version would not have been possible without the encouragement and guidance of my niece, Wren Handman, who suggested that I elaborate on various subjects and reorganize the contents. She provided her excellent editing skills for a far better read. I am extremely grateful for all her assistance as well as her availability whenever I asked for her advice.

I owe thanks to Jenny Lorentowicz, who made extensive corrections throughout my first draft, as well as to Carle Jane Evans and Louise Samson for reading and commenting on my text. I also wish to thank my brother Marcus for his encouragement when, after reading my book, he told me that "it was a good read." I appreciate the time spent by my sister-in-law Gwendolyn Maroon, who suggested a number of changes in my text. I also appreciate the constructive comments of the other members of my family who read my text—namely, my nephew Misha Handman, my brother Jim Handman, and my sister-in-law Renee Pellerin.

Special thanks go to Julius Grey, who read my memoir with a legal eye to ensure correctness.

Huge thanks to Josephine Mo, Acquisitions Editor, and the editorial team at University of Toronto Press for giving me the opportunity to tell my story to readers who want to know all about judging. I wish to acknowledge Stacy Belden, my copy editor, who corrected my spelling errors and footnotes and ensured proper style throughout. I also wish to thank those who worked to edit, design, typeset, and launch my book.

Introduction

"Objection!" the lawyer exclaims loudly, as his opponent tries to submit a new document to the court. "Objection dismissed," the judge answers without waiting for the opposing lawyer's response. The trial quickly wraps up, and the judge renders a decision from the bench. The judge bangs a gavel on his tabletop. The case is over!

This is drama. It is the type of scenario seen on television or in the movies. It is not what takes place in actual courtrooms. There are many misconceptions about the law. For most people, courtrooms are mysterious places, and the legal jargon is incomprehensible. During my time on the bench, I was constantly asked:

How did you become a judge?
What is it like being a judge?
What kind of judge are you?
Are you tough?
How can you tell who is telling the truth?

These questions were the impetus for me to write this book. It was evident from the questions I received that people were intrigued and interested in many aspects of my job—from how I obtained the position to how I exercised my functions. I knew that I could dispel some of the myths about our justice system while sharing the story of my time on the bench.

This book takes readers behind the scenes and provides an inside look at the inner workings of the justice system. It shares my personal story from the time I wished to go into law until the present time. It describes the role of a judge and explains the various aspects a judge considers in a trial, including objections, expert witnesses, and evidence, and how judges deal with conflicting versions of a story. The book describes many cases I heard at the Court of Quebec. A number are detailed because the subject matter was particularly interesting (the motorcycle theft), unusual (fraud), or complex (the violation of a lawyer's *Code of Ethics*).[1] I elaborate on some cases in the Small Claims Court as well as the challenge of maintaining decorum and running a hearing when the parties are not represented by lawyers and have little or no knowledge of the law.

Other cases were those heard in "chambers" where individuals may be confined to an institution or granted a restricted driver's licence. When I acted as a mediator, my role was to assist warring parties reach a settlement. In addition, the book deals with complaints against judges, the activities of the court, and the people involved. Although I sat on three different tribunals during my career, including two labour tribunals, nearly all the cases described come from the Civil Division of the Court of Quebec. These cases have a more general interest, while the concepts in my cases dealing with labour issues are complex and are only of interest to those involved in that area of the law.

Chapter 1

1 *Code of Professional Conduct of Lawyers*, CQLR c B-1, r 3.1.

I wrote the book "Madam Justice" for the public to provide an idea of what it was like to sit on the bench. However, lawyers, law professors, and students may also be curious about various aspects of the work of a judge. While judgments provide the facts of a case, the parties' positions, and the applicable law, they do not tell the whole story. This book does. In explaining what goes into reaching a decision, readers will understand that judges have a true concern to render a judgment that is correct in law and, whenever possible, one that is equitable. I hope this book provides readers with a glimpse of the inner workings of the justice system and how justice is rendered.

There are few books written by Canadian judges. Most judges are more comfortable in pursuing the process of their decision making out of the public eye. As the justice writer Sean Fine wrote in the *Globe and Mail* on 22 October 2019 in his article entitled "Through the Eyes of the Law," referring to the judges of the Supreme Court of Canada: "Most Supreme Court judges in Canada are unknown to most Canadians. And mostly, judges seem to like it that way. They give lots of speeches, but mostly 'in house' to lawyers' groups and law students. . . . In anonymity, there is less of a public spotlight on one's judicial choices." The same comment can be made about judges who sit on lower courts. However, I believe it is important for judges to be more transparent so that the work of judges and our justice system are not a mystery.

Virtually all judges are selected from amongst lawyers who studied law and then began practising. My path to the bench, however, was not a straight line.

Chapter 1

The Beginning

My personal assistant, Pat Melvin, buzzed my telephone line. She sounded rather puzzled. "There's a woman on line one who would like to speak to you. She says that she's calling on behalf of someone named Madam Linda Goupil. Do you want to take the call?" Pat asked. My heart skipped a beat. Of course, I would take the call. Pat did not know who the caller was. However, I did. Unbeknownst to Pat, I had applied for a position as a judge on the Quebec Labour Court. Madam Goupil was the minister of justice in the province of Quebec at that time and the person who would ultimately decide my fate.

It was April 2000. I was living in Ottawa where I held the position of vice-chair on the Canada Labour Relations Board, with a mandate of ten years. I was anxious to return home to Montreal. My mother, Eunice, was a widow and alone in that city. I wanted a permanent position—particularly, one as a judge in the field of labour law, the field of law that I had practised as a lawyer and that I thoroughly enjoyed. And, finally, but not necessarily in that order, I had met a man named Bjørn Ellingsen. He lived in Montreal, and I hoped to see more of him.

Madam Goupil's representative informed me that I was on the shortlist for the opening on the Quebec Labour

Court. She asked whether there was anything I wished to divulge that could disqualify me as a judge. I quickly racked my brain but could only think of one fact: "Well, I was given a speeding ticket as I drove to Montreal from Ottawa on one of my many trips back and forth between the two cities." Since she did not ask for the details, I did not offer any—I was not eager to divulge how fast I had been driving. She thanked me for the information and said that I would be notified as to the government's decision in the near future.

I could not concentrate for the rest of the day. Early in the afternoon, I left my office. As I passed Pat's desk, I mumbled that I planned to work on my current case at home. This was not unusual as I often drafted decisions from home. I hoped that by concentrating on a draft of a recent case, I would be able to put the phone call out of my mind. However, to my astonishment, I received a phone call from the minister of justice herself that very afternoon. Madam Goupil informed me that I had been named as a judge on the Quebec Labour Court and congratulated me. She reminded me that I must remain humble and carry out my duties with dignity and integrity. I kept repeating, "*Merci, merci*" and "*Bien sûr*" ("Thank you, thank you" and "Of course"). Our brief conversation took place in French, and I was afraid to say more. My fluency in that language had decreased over the years I had spent in Ottawa since I mostly heard cases in English. I was afraid that if I said too much in less than fluent French, she would revoke my appointment.

I felt as if I had won a lottery, and, in many ways, I had. Being a judge comes with various privileges: prestige, status, an excellent salary, an interesting and challenging job, and a generous pension. Being a judge also encompasses responsibilities, which I was more than ready to assume. Since I had been presiding over cases for several years, I felt ready for this position and the new challenges involved. I thought back to my youth and marvelled at the path my life had taken, a path that I had never imagined.

GROWING UP WITHOUT GOOGLE

The name I was given at birth was Susan Merle Gersovitch. I bear none of those names now. My biological father, Jack Gersovitch, passed away when I was six months old. My mother, Eunice Freeman, remarried Stanley Handman, who was her brother's best friend. Stanley had met my mother many years before when she was about eighteen years old. He told her that he was going off to war but would marry her when he returned. "Don't be silly," my mother's replied. "I'm not going to wait for you. I'll be married by then." It turned out that they were both right.

While Stanley was in the army, my mother married another man and then became a widow. Stanley returned, married my mother, and adopted me as his own. My family name became Handman. I changed my first names many years later when I was told that I would be required to use my legal name in my practice of law. I decided that I preferred my name to be "Suzanne" since that was what I was called by my friends. I dropped my middle name, and Suzanne officially became my first name.

When I was growing up, my father was very strict. He was concerned about how his children spoke and wrote, and he emphasized the proper use of the English language at all times. When I was young and wrote letters home from camp, he even went as far as to correct them in red ink. Although I was outraged by his attention to such details, I did learn how to write. Little did I realize at the time that learning to write in a clear and concise manner would be a most useful asset in my career.

I was always a perfectionist and a type A personality. According to my late mother, when I made a mistake in writing a text, I would recopy the entire page rather than cross out the mistake. Of course, this was before word processors. I eventually stopped that behaviour, but I have remained a perfectionist, striving to excel.

I consider my upbringing to have been ordinary. Perhaps what was distinctive was the intellectual and leftist bent of our household as well as the many books, magazines, and newspapers that filled our house. Amongst the most important values in our household were learning and education. It is not unusual for families to argue, and my family was no different. However, while many families argue over who left the cap off the toothpaste tube, the arguments in our family centred on current events, social issues, and social justice, such as whether there was grassroots democracy in India, whether a socialist system was appropriate for an under-developed country, and whether it was appropriate for garbage collectors to earn as much as they did. (My parents pointed out that few people were interested in doing such work, and it was only proper that garbage collectors be well paid.) After supper, one of us was almost always sent upstairs to our library to get the encyclopedia to resolve the discussion that was taking place around the dining room table. Google would have been most helpful at that time.

A CIRCUITOUS PATH TO LAW

I didn't grow up with the dream of becoming a judge. In fact, I did not even dream about becoming a lawyer. I had read a biography about Marie Curie when I was very young and wanted to become a famous scientist, as she was. Later, toward the end of high school, I told my father that I did not want to go to university. He replied that I could sweep floors in a five and dime store as long as I first obtained a university degree. There was no question of me not attending university. I was expected to continue my education, become a professional, and succeed in my chosen field.

It was not until I was an undergraduate at McGill University in the 1960s that I began to think about graduate school and considered law as a career possibility. The idea first began by a process of elimination. I was not good enough in mathematics to go into engineering or architecture; my hands were not steady enough to become a dentist; and I had little interest in accounting or most other professions. On the other hand, I found the law students I dated to be far more interesting than those who were studying in other fields. The subjects they were studying were compelling.

Unfortunately, when I raised the possibility of becoming a lawyer with my father, he was vehemently opposed to the idea. He insisted that law was not a profession for a woman and tried to steer me toward medicine. His reaction was not unusual. At the time I had planned to attend graduate school, there were only two women who had entered law school at McGill University—ever—and only one of the women had graduated. I was undeterred. Law, I felt sure, was the path for me. My father, having failed to dissuade me, involved my uncle Harold Freeman in the discussions. Harold, who was a lawyer, told me there was no point in earning my degree. He believed that I could graduate and do well in law school but that there would be no job waiting for me. As a woman in a male-dominated field, he was convinced that no one would hire me. It would be preferable, he said, to consider another career.

Discouraged by what I felt was a voice of experience, I agreed to pursue another career. I graduated with a degree in audiology and worked first as a clinical audiologist and then as a professor in audiology at the University of Montreal. When I spearheaded the movement to found a professor's union at the university, our fledging organization hired Helen Lebel, a labour lawyer, to help us obtain union certification. Through the course of the meetings that we had with her, I developed an understanding of labour organizations and how they functioned. My fascination with labour relations was far greater than my interest in audiology. I was inspired to return to my idea of practising law. Little did I know then that my career would, to a certain extent, mirror that of Helen Lebel's career.

I applied and was admitted to the law faculty at McGill University. I was thrilled, but when I told my family, my uncle Harold, who had finally accepted the fact that I was determined to become a lawyer, insisted that I go to the University of Montreal and study in French rather than in English. He explained that it was important to learn the law in French since I would have to use it in my practice. He also claimed that the University of Montreal was a much friendlier environment. His second argument was particularly compelling. According to rumour, the competition at McGill was so fierce that students tore pages out of books in the law library in order to have an advantage over their classmates. Whether or not that rumour was actually true, I accepted his advice and decided that I would attend the University of Montreal.

I enjoyed the study of law. The students, on the average, were approximately ten years younger than I was and had come to law school straight out of junior college or university, with little idea as to the nature of the career they had chosen. I, on the contrary, had very definite ideas and a definite goal. I was not studying law simply to become a lawyer. Because of my experience in labour relations as a professor at the University of Montreal, I had already decided that I wanted to become a labour lawyer and represent unions and employees. Even before graduating, I applied to the firm Trudel Nadeau, one of the best-known labour law firms in Canada. There were no openings at that time, but I was not discouraged. I applied to several other firms and was accepted at more than one large, prestigious law firm. I wanted to practise labour law, but, with that avenue temporarily cut off, I wound up working in real estate and customs law.

Although I was not happy with these assignments, one memorable assignment involved a customs case that was to be heard by the Senate of Canada. I had worked extensively on the file and was sent by a senior lawyer to observe other cases at the Senate and report back to him. To my dismay, when I arrived at the Senate, I was told that our case would proceed in half an hour and a postponement was not possible. This was before the time of smartphones, and I was unable to reach the partner who was responsible for the file.

Since I had written the brief to be presented to the Senate and was very familiar with all the issues involved, I presented our client's position before the chamber. I responded to the questions posed without difficulty. To my surprise, I was not nervous at all. Perhaps it was because the invitation to address the Senate took place so quickly. When I returned to the firm, the partner responsible for the file was furious that I had presented the case without him. Of course, his ire cooled when we subsequently learned that I had won our case. I was delighted with the outcome.

Not long after that, I was unexpectedly given the chance to plead a labour law case against a lawyer from the law firm Trudel Nadeau, the very same firm where I had dreamed about practising labour law. To my astonishment, I won the case. Shortly after, I saw an advertisement for a position at the firm and applied. Although I did not have the requisite experience that the firm was seeking, I pleaded with the managing partner to give me a chance. After several interviews, I managed to convince the partners to hire me.

THE PRACTICE OF LABOUR LAW

Shortly after I had begun working at the law firm of Trudel Nadeau, I received a phone call from an individual who told me he was seeking a lawyer to assist a ship, which was being held in the harbour, to leave the country. I was told that the ship had been detained for dealing in arms, which were destined for Cuba. I called the consulate to obtain further information. The person I spoke with—in my Spanish, which was far from perfect—assured me that there was no ship travelling to Cuba from Montreal. He had no idea what I was talking about. I tried very hard to explain what the problem was but made no headway. I was anxious that I had bungled the very first assignment I had been given.

Then I heard noise outside my office door. I opened the door and found several of the lawyers engulfed in laughter.

The assignment was a prank. They explained that they had succeeded to *monter un bateau*, which literally means to "build a ship" but is a French expression that means "to fool someone." My colleagues worked hard but could also be playful and have fun.

I was delighted to finally be practising labour law, which was the area of law I had hoped to work in. I recall one of the first arbitration cases that I pleaded at the beginning of my career. When I began to present my arguments and started citing jurisprudence, the arbitrator said it was not necessary to present those cases; they were all well known. My client exclaimed: "You may know the cases, but my lawyer is just beginning her career and she wants to show what she knows!" His remarks elicited laughter from everyone at the hearing, but I was mortified.

There is much to learn at the outset of a law practice. During a hearing of one of my initial arbitration cases, I asked the opposite party a question. Before he could answer, the arbitrator asked me why I was asking that question. He pointed out that no one had contradicted my client's evidence, which could happen if I gave the other party a chance to explain his position. I quickly withdrew my question. I won my case and learned an important lesson—namely, to choose my questions carefully and to consider the impact of what I asked.

One mandate that was ultimately very important to my career was a case that involved maritime law—this time for real. I was told in the morning that a group of sailors were in the port of Montreal and had not been paid their wages. My job was to seize the ship to obtain their unpaid wages. I assured the union representative that I would take care of the problem, although I had no idea how to seize a ship or anything else for that matter. Counsel for the shipping company called me to try to negotiate a settlement, but it was not going well. I learned that the ship would be leaving port before midnight, and I feared that, if no settlement was reached at that time, my clients would not be paid. On the advice of another lawyer I knew, I asked several lawyers in our firm to prepare an application for an order from the Federal Court of Canada to seize the ship while I continued to negotiate with the opposing lawyer who represented the shipping company.

Late in the evening, the opposing lawyer announced that there could be no agreement and that the ship would be leaving Montreal in less than two hours. I immediately set my plan into action. The necessary court order had come through hours before, and we were ready. I contacted a bailiff to seize the ship by serving the court order on the ship's captain, on the ship's mast, on the harbour master, on the ship pilot, on the port authorities, and the other required recipients. The ship was unable to leave the port.

The following day, the captain came to our firm with a suitcase full of money. It felt like a scene in a movie. The operation was a success. The sailors received their wages, and I was made a partner of the law firm.

I practised law at Trudel Nadeau for twelve years. It afforded me the appropriate experience and background for the remainder of my labour law career. Our small intimate law firm merged on several occasions, and, following each merger, the firm necessarily increased in size. Although I had become a partner, I did not move up the ranks with more junior lawyers below me; instead, the senior partners of the other firms who had joined Trudel Nadeau assumed a higher hierarchical position than I had. Our firm became more structured and more formal.

Instead of walking into another office to inform a fellow lawyer of some event, notices were sent out to each of us. I began to think about greener pastures.

It was time for a change.

LABOUR LAW ACROSS THE COUNTRY

I applied for a position as a vice-chair of the Canada Labour Relations Board in Ottawa.[1] In the past, I had applied for other positions by submitting my curriculum vitae and meeting with the persons involved in the hiring process. However, I had never lobbied for a position. Looking back, I am not sure how I decided what I had to do to obtain a position that was, in essence, a political appointment.[2] I somehow just knew that I needed someone to vouch for me.

Many people maintain that it is not fair to have others lobby on one's behalf. I agree in theory, but, in practice, since that was what other "political" candidates were doing, I wanted to level the playing field. At the same time, I felt comfortable submitting my candidature. I was a partner in one of the most highly regarded labour law firms not only in the province of Quebec but also in Canada. I had the necessary credentials for the job I sought.

I began by contacting several people I knew and even some I didn't know personally, including my member of parliament and a person I had met on a holiday who had since then become a cabinet minister. I even contacted a few female cabinet ministers who did not know me but who I hoped would support me in my attempt to be named

1 This tribunal is now called the Canada Industrial Relations Board.

2 This position was a Governor in Council appointment, and the occupants of such positions serve at the pleasure of the government.

to the board. When one minister told me that she had already undertaken to support another candidate, I persisted and asked if she would at least accept my curriculum vitae and consider my application. I forwarded my application to her despite her reservations.

I do not know who was most influential in my quest to obtain this nomination, but my strategy paid off. I was named as a vice-chair of the Canada Labour Relations Board. The day I received the good news, my father had a heart attack. Unfortunately, he passed away a week later and did not get to see my swearing-in ceremony or follow my career, which was so important to him. I often wondered whether the excitement about my new job had anything to do with it. Friends who came to visit me following the funeral and at the *shiva*[3] asked what was appropriate to express: their congratulations or their sympathies. The answer was obvious to me: both were appropriate.

My position as vice-chair was a ten-year appointment that involved deciding labour cases across Canada. I did not have the title of judge but, rather, was called "madam president" when I presided over hearings. The work involved essentially the same aspects as that of a judge: studying a file, hearing evidence and legal arguments, deciding the outcome, and writing a decision. The main difference was that our salary was considerably higher than that of the judges on the Quebec Labour Court. Apparently, the federal government's pay scales were more generous than those of the Quebec government.

3 The *shiva* is the period of mourning in the Jewish religion beginning immediately after the funeral service and burial. The family members of the deceased gather to mourn their loss and receive condolences from relatives and friends.

When I arrived at the Canada Labour Relations Board, the chairperson requested that I participate as a member of a panel that he chaired rather than preside over the hearing since it was my first case on the board. After the case was heard, the chairperson asked me and the other panel member to meet with him the following morning. When I came to the meeting, I was dismayed to discover that he did not want to discuss the case. Rather, he had decided its outcome already and had even drafted a decision ready for our consideration. It appeared that the chairperson had assumed that I would readily agree with the outcome he had reached. I told him that I wanted time to review both the evidence and his draft and left the meeting with the documentation and his draft decision in hand. Since the subject matter concerned an alleged illegal strike, a decision had to be rendered quickly.

I studied the file and decided that I did not agree with the chairperson (or the other member of the panel who had agreed to sign the decision as written). For me, the anticipated strike was lawful since the workers had lawfully acquired a right to strike. My conclusion meant that I would have to write a dissenting opinion. I did so very quickly. The situation that ensued was interesting. No one on the board, before that, had ever written a dissent, and the communications department was not certain how to handle my decision. I had just arrived on the board and immediately had created a stir. Ultimately, the board published the majority decision, followed by my dissent. This set a precedent, and many other board members wrote dissents after that.

The Canada Labour Relations Board heard cases involving unions and companies in the private sector all over the country. Our cases dealt with all aspects of collective bargaining from union certification applications and bad faith bargaining to strikes and lockouts. While our headquarters were in Ottawa, we presided over hearings in the location where each complaint or application was filed. As a result, I sat in towns and cities throughout Canada from the East Coast to the West Coast and in the far North. I had a suitcase that was always ready to go. It was not unusual for me to fly out of Ottawa on a Monday and return by Thursday evening. Sometimes, we would get a file in the morning that was urgent. Whoever was presiding over that case, together with two board members and a clerk, would board a plane that same afternoon. On occasion, one of the lawyers from the board's legal department accompanied us to a hearing. During my time in office, I learned even more about labour law.

After having represented unions and employees in my law practice, I found it challenging, at first, to consider the conflict from the employer's side as well. Ultimately, however, hearing both parties and deciding the outcome of a case was far more interesting for me than litigating on behalf of clients. I gained experience in running a hearing with two opposing parties as well as a hearing encompassing multiple parties, and I wrote numerous decisions.

Toward the end of my time at the Canada Labour Relations Board, I also became involved in mediating disputes, even before receiving formal training in this area. The work was stimulating and exciting. What was most interesting was the fact that, as a board, we were establishing policy in the area of labour law that impacted labour relations across Canada. The years I spent at the board were memorable and provided me with the necessary experience to later assume a position as a judge on the Quebec Labour Court.

Unfortunately, after less than five years in Ottawa, my career at the Canada Labour Relations Board came to a crashing end: the government decided to eliminate the board and create another in its place.[4] It was renamed the Canada Industrial Relations Board. A few provisions of the *Canada Labour Code* were modified, but it remained essentially the same in its mission and in the type of cases it handled.[5] What changed was a salary reduction for the vice-chair and a term that was reduced from ten years to five, both of which significantly impacted upon the position and made it less desirable.

While I was completing my cases after the new board was created, I noted that a position had become available on the Quebec Labour Court. I was ecstatic. After my experience on the Canada Labour Relations Board, a position as a judge in Quebec had become my dream job. I immediately submitted my application. I advised many people in Quebec that I wanted to obtain the position as judge on the Quebec Labour Court. I even approached a couple of cabinet ministers at a wedding. While this was not the appropriate time to lobby for a job, I realized that I might never have another chance to speak to anyone who might be influential in the appointment process. I also asked others to lobby on my behalf. I am not certain where I learned how to be my own advocate; I had no mentor. But I was determined to do whatever I could to get the only job I genuinely wanted.

The application process has changed since those days. At the time of writing, for federal appointments to the

4 A dispute with the chairperson arose over the assignment of cases and generated negative publicity, which the government did not appreciate. As a result, the government sought a more compliant board.

5 *Canada Labour Code*, RSC 1985, c L-2.

Supreme Court[6] and the Court of Appeal of each province, candidates are required to keep their applications confidential, presumably to eliminate lobbying activity and to level the playing field. Following a review by a judicial advisory committee, recommendations are made to the justice minister. No interviews are held. For the Court of Quebec, applicants are now also required to keep their applications confidential. The change that took place in Quebec stemmed from the recommendations of the Bastarache Commission,[7] which held an inquiry on the process for appointing the judges of the Court of Quebec and other provincial tribunals. The commission sought to improve the appointment process by eliminating the influence of parties and making it more transparent.

The new appointment process was not in effect when I applied to become a judge on the Quebec Labour Court. While there was no prohibition to lobby at that time, the selection of the successful candidate nevertheless entailed an interview by a committee that included the chief justice of that court. Following the interview process, a shortlist of three candidates was recommended to the minister of justice, who would then select the successful candidate for the available position. Consequently, one had to succeed in the interview to be considered. Knowing this, I went to great lengths to prepare for the interview.

6 The court, which is known in the other provinces as the Supreme Court, is called the Superior Court in Quebec.

7 "No Evidence of Influence Peddling: Bastarache," *CBC News* (19 January 2011), online: <www.cbc.ca/news/canada/montreal/no-evidence-of-influence-peddling-bastarache-1.1066274> (the Bastarache Commission found there was no evidence of influence peddling).

Chapter 2

Becoming a Judge

It was clear to me that many lawyers would be applying for the opening on the Quebec Labour Court, and, virtually, all of them would be experienced labour law practitioners. I wanted some means of standing out, other than my English accent. I spent considerable time studying pertinent Quebec legislation and reading the province's *Labour Code* and related legislation.[1] I also read several books, one of which was entitled *Le droit de l'emploi au Québec*.[2] It turned out to be the most important text that I read in my preparations, although I had no means of knowing it before the interview.

During the time I was at the Canada Labour Relations Board, I was assigned cases primarily in English. Some of my francophone colleagues, unjustifiably, claimed they could not follow a case that was not in their native language. As a result, my spoken French became somewhat rusty. As soon as I realized this, I insisted that all of my conversations and communications with my francophone colleagues and friends be in French. I also signed up for

Chapter 2

1 *Labour Code*, CQLR c C-27.

2 Fernand Morin et al, *Le droit de l'emploi au Québec*, 4th ed (Montreal: Wilson & Lafleur, 2010).

training given by an outsourcing firm that assisted people to find appropriate employment and prepare for interviews. Our main topic of conversation? What I would wear: a black suit or a red suit. The idea of the red suit was to ensure that the interviewers would remember me. The black suit, on the other hand, was appropriate given the conservative nature of a judge's position. We decided that the interviewers, in all probability, would remember me since anglophone labour lawyers were few and far between. I settled on the black suit.

I was coached, videoed, and subjected to positive criticism. "Retain eye contact," my coach told me. "Don't fidget with papers, maintain the same level of enthusiasm for all the subjects you discuss, don't get flustered if you don't know the response." Finally, my coach said: "Whenever you can, turn a negative into a positive." The advice to turn a negative into a positive was the most valuable advice I could have received.

I arrived early for the interview, which took place at the Labour Court, and no matter how well I had prepared for the event, I was nervous. I was called into the interview room and seated facing three people: the chief justice, a member of the Quebec Bar Association, and a well-known labour lawyer. The three men were formally dressed and appeared very serious. To relieve my tension, I told the group that I was used to sitting in their place and making the decisions rather than the other way around. "It's a little uncomfortable changing places!" That brought about a chuckle and helped lessen my nerves.

I was ready for the interview. I expected questions such as "Why do you want to be a judge?" or "What are your strengths and weaknesses?"; in other words, the usual questions in an interview. Instead, I faced no generalities.

The questions dealt with various aspects of labour law and, to my surprise, included questions about various laws in the province of Ontario rather than Quebec.

What I recall most was a question dealing with penal law. I had been dreading any questions in this area since I had never practised penal law and had little knowledge of the field. Sure enough, when faced with a question on this topic, I had no idea what the correct response was. I felt a momentary flush of panic. However, I recalled the precious advice I had received from my outsourcing coach: turn a negative into a positive.

As it happened, the lawyer who was on the interview panel was Jean-Yves Brière, one of the authors of the text *Le droit de l'emploi au Québec*, which contained a chapter on penal law. I calmly stated that I did not know the answer to the question since I had not had the opportunity to practise in that area, but I had read the chapter on that subject in the lawyer's text. Adding to that, I explained that I learned quickly. I related the example of having successfully seized a ship for the wages of sailors when I was a lawyer, although I had no idea that this could even be done when I received the mandate in the morning of the seizure. My response appeared to satisfy the panel. I had followed the advice of my coach, and it had worked.

Four months passed after my interview with no news about the outcome of my application. I became less and less optimistic about the possibility of becoming a judge. During this time, I applied and interviewed for a job as a coroner. While my interview went very well, and I later learned that I was one of the few finalists for that position, it was not my first choice for employment. Then, suddenly, I received the phone call from Quebec's minister of labour, who advised me that I had been chosen as a judge on the Quebec Labour Court. To say that I was elated is an understatement. I could not have been happier. My appointment was one of the highlights of my life.

SWORN IN

My swearing in ceremony took place in the springtime. I had two concerns beforehand. The first and most obvious was the speech that I was expected to present. My other concern was that, since judges on the Labour Court did not wear a *toge* (which, in English, we call a robe), I was told that I should wear something sober, such as a dark suit. While I had been working at the Canada Labour Relations Board, I had worn suits that were less formal than what was expected for the ceremony, and the dark suit worn at my interview was too ordinary, so I did not have one that was suitable for the occasion.

I began searching for the perfect black suit. I tried on many, but, in each one, I felt that I looked as if I was going to a funeral. I was relieved when I finally found an appropriate—but extremely expensive—suit at an exclusive store called Julius Richardson's in Ottawa. I was told that Aline, the wife of then Prime Minister Jean Chrétien, had bought the same suit. I hoped that we would not meet each other while wearing our Julius Richardson outfits. Since I was returning to live in Montreal, and, at that time, she lived in Ottawa, I assumed there would be little chance of that happening.

As for my speech, I had been to a number of swearing-in ceremonies where I had heard speeches. The problem was that I remembered little from any of them. The only one that had stuck with me was one that detailed the family life of the newly appointed judge in a most interesting manner. While I understood that my presentation was to deal in a concise way with my family, my background, and my concerns as a labour court judge, it was important for me to provide details that would make my story both human and interesting. So I set out to emulate the one speech that I recalled.

In talking about my early years, I related how I remembered my mother walking around the house with a paintbrush in her hand while one of my brothers was ironing his pants. I also talked about the importance of all forms of art in my household and of the ballet, theatre, and music lessons that I was given. I made the whole room laugh when I shared the fact that I played the violin so badly that I was relegated to practising in the basement with a mute on my violin. I spoke about my experience as a labour lawyer and, subsequently, as a vice-chair of the Canada Labour Relations Board. I shared my thoughts about the changes taking place in labour relations, including the new jurisdiction over pay equity and various unresolved issues at that time, such as the accessibility of labour regimes and other relevant matters. I considered it a privilege and an honour to have been appointed to the Labour Court and to play a role in the challenges that lay ahead, and I expressed my gratitude for the opportunity to do so.

It was not difficult to put my ideas on paper. I had learned that from my father, Stanley. Writing my speech in French was more of a challenge. I ended up presenting it partly in French and partly in English. Since I was the first anglophone judge named to the Labour Court, I was obviously the first to present any part of a speech in English.

The ceremony was small and relatively intimate. It took place at the Labour Court, which was situated in the northeast part of Montreal and did not have a large space for such an event. This was in contrast to the swearing-in ceremony of judges at the main courthouse of Montreal, which has room for several hundred persons. I was warned in advance that space was limited, and, accordingly, my guest list was somewhat short.

Bernard Lesage, the chief justice of the Labour Court,[3] spoke about my appointment, clearly expressing his approval for the diversity I was bringing to the court. Other speakers included a member of the judges' association from the Court of Quebec, a member of the bar of Montreal, and one of my friends. The member of the bar of Montreal, who I presume would prefer to remain anonymous, had incorrectly noted the time of the event and arrived when it was over. He apologized profusely and gave me a copy of his presentation. It was very well written and humorous; I was sorry he had not been present at the ceremony to deliver it.

My friend Chantal was also designated to give a speech. I know that she was happy that I had obtained the position, but, at the same time, she was upset that I was leaving Ottawa. Not only were we good friends, but she was living in my house at the time. Given her emotions, she found it difficult to speak. She nevertheless was able to roast me on some of my idiosyncrasies, and I appreciated her heartfelt comments.

I was warmly received by the chief justice and my new colleagues. The Labour Court arranged for a cocktail party for all those present. It was a joyous occasion for me, but I was nevertheless somewhat on edge: my mother Eunice, who I was very close to and who had come to celebrate my appointment, had begun to develop dementia and was not totally functional. Eunice was a diminutive

---

3 Judge Bernard Lesage passed away several years ago. I liked him and admired him immensely and regret his passing.

woman, who in her later years wore bold makeup and bright, printed dresses. I made sure that she was appropriately dressed and made up for this occasion. At one point, I noticed her talking to the chief justice. The two were sitting in a quiet part of the reception area, and their heads were tilted in close. Their body language was animated. They appeared to be deep in conversation.

I recalled how upset I had been about a conversation we had had before my swearing in ceremony. I had consulted her about a renovation project for the home I had bought. After detailing the options that I had for the entrance, I asked her for her opinion about the best colour for the floor tiles. Despite my lengthy explanation and the samples that I had shown her of the wall colours and the floor tiles, she had not been able to follow the conversation. When I asked her: "What do you think is the best option?" she replied: "What option are you talking about?" It was natural, then, that I would be worried about what she was saying to the chief justice. However, I did not need to be concerned. She had hidden her illness for several years and managed to do so again that day. Judge Lesage told me that he found her to be charming. I was so relieved.

It was difficult for me that my father had already passed away and could not be there to see my swearing in. My father had more ambition for me than I had for myself. While he initially opposed my desire to get a law degree, when I did become a lawyer, he asked when I would become a partner in my law firm. When I became a partner, he asked when I would become a judge. Since he pushed me to excel, I owe my career, in part, to his high expectations. It would have meant so much to him, and to me, for him to see me sworn in as a judge.

My career as a judge took unexpected turns, including a transfer to a division of the Court of Quebec that involved the interpretation and application of different laws. The learning curve was steep, but, ultimately, I learned a great deal. I gained valuable information not only for my varied court cases but also for so many situations in everyday life. After I retired from the bench, I continued to mediate, speak at conferences around the world, and even published a book called *Mediation for Lawyers: A Practical Guide for Effective Representation of Your Clients*.[4]

My personal life also changed during my time at the Quebec Labour Court in wonderful ways and in tragic ones. It not only included my move back to Montreal, which suited me very well, but also a new relationship that would go on to become a strong, happy marriage.

Unfortunately, not everything was so happy. Near the beginning of my tenure at the Court of Quebec, my mother went to the hospital for what I thought was a minor problem. I expected her stay to be a short one. However, she developed C-difficile and unexpectedly passed away. I had been extremely close to her and was devastated by her passing. While she was in the hospital, I was there with her nearly every day. I continued to hear my assigned cases but was unable to write my judgments until sometime later. Everyone involved at the Labour Court was very understanding. I will always appreciate the lack of pressure and the support I received from my chief justice during that dark period of my life.

The rest of this book details my court cases and my life both in court and outside court.

---

4 Suzanne Handman, *Mediation for Lawyers: A Practical Guide for Effective Representation of Your Clients* (Toronto: Irwin Law, 2024).

Chapter 3

The Quebec Labour Court

I began my career as a judge at the Quebec Labour Court, a small, specialized tribunal that was separate from the main courthouse in Montreal, which was in another part of the city. This court was one of several in the province.

The Municipal Court hears contestations to parking and speeding tickets, offences to the Highway Safety Code, and minor criminal matters, while the Court of Quebec deals with civil law, commercial law, criminal law, and cases dealing with young offenders and youth protection. The Superior Court of Quebec (called the Supreme Court in other provinces) is a higher court, which hears civil and commercial cases, including family law and bankruptcy, as well as criminal law. Decisions of both the Court of Quebec and the Superior Court can be appealed to the Court of Appeal. Each of these courts holds hearings. However, the trials are very different from those portrayed on television and in the movies. They are longer, far more complex, and far less dramatic than the scenarios created for viewers.

My time at the Quebec Labour Court was a happy period because of the collegiality among the judges and my comfort in judging the cases I heard. They dealt with the usual type of labour issues: certification of unions, bad faith negotiations, strikes and lockouts, unfair labour practices, and so on. Unfortunately, my stay at this court was short-lived. The Quebec Labour Court was abolished a few years after my arrival, and I was transferred to another court.

REAL TRIALS VERSUS DRAMA

Courtroom scenes on television or in the movies make me crazy. I rant and rave as the scene progresses. Of course, in a television program or a movie, a trial cannot continue for days; instead, a limited slice of a trial is shown on the screen. Even within those constraints, however, the details are often completely wrong. For example, a lawyer yells "Objection," and, without hearing what the opposing side has to say about the issue, the judge rules on the objection. At the same time that I am complaining: "The judge didn't give the opposite party a chance to rebut the objection!" my husband is telling me to "shush" because he is trying to listen to the scene.

Another common media trope is that lawyers come to court with documentary evidence that their opponent not only has never seen but also did not know existed. There is no second copy of the document for that party—only one copy exists—and it is given to the judge. The opposite party is taken completely by surprise. This does not happen in actual cases. Parties must provide the opposing party with a written account of their case; they must also provide a copy of their exhibits and of the reports of their experts if they intend to present any experts at the hearing. We do not have the surprise attacks that take place as they do so often in dramas. In the event that a party attempts to produce evidence for the first time at trial that the opposite party was not aware of, with few exceptions, it will not be admissible.

Fictional cross examinations on television or in the movies are even more dramatic. Every lawyer is so skilled that, within an extremely short period of time, the lawyer manages to put the opposite party or one of the witnesses of the opposing party into a corner. The lawyer then succeeds in getting that party, or the witness, to make a contradictory statement or, even better (against the party's own interest), admit to an essential fact in the case. The lawyer successfully establishes what the lawyer has set out to prove, and, no matter how complex the case, the judge always renders a decision from the bench immediately after the arguments are presented. The case is over quickly.

The scenario I have just described never happens in a real courtroom. When I sat on the Quebec Labour Court, my trials most often took several days. Cases at the Court of Quebec lasted on average between one and five days. Exceptionally, one of my cases was heard over a period of ten days. The duration of cases in Superior Court often extends over many days or weeks and, in some cases, the trial can go on for months. In court, the story unfolds slowly, and many witnesses are heard. In fact, some cases can be very tedious as each witness describes the same event in minute detail. The closing arguments may also take considerable time as the lawyers not only summarize the facts but also point to the legal basis for their case, submit case law, and read lengthy passages aloud from various cases. It is no wonder why fiction chooses not to represent trials in a completely accurate way. It does not make for a gripping scene.

Many people are not aware of the fact that the public has access to court trials. With the exception of a few types of cases that are held *in camera*—that is, they are private—anyone can enter a courtroom and watch a proceeding in court. Attending a hearing might dispel the misconceptions that people have about our court system. I encourage people to attend at least one case in their lifetime.

LABOUR LAW IN THE PROVINCE

The Labour Court was very different from the Canada Labour Relations Board in many ways. My new offices were located in an old building in the north end of Montreal. Contrary to the board's spacious wood-panelled and well-furnished offices, our offices were sparse and basic, and we did not have the large support staff that we had at the board. We each had an assistant, while a single legal researcher and an information technology assistant who was not continually present on site were available to assist all of us.

On the other hand, there was little formality. When I wished to speak with Bernard Lesage, our chief justice, I knocked on his door, which was usually open, walked in, and sat down. He was always available to discuss a case, any issue of concern to me, or some political event that had arisen. I thoroughly enjoyed our discussions. The lack of formality at the Labour Court extended to the staff. There was one lunchroom that was shared by the judges and our assistants. We did not have the hierarchy that exists in other courts where the judges' dining room is restricted to judges.

Since I had replaced a judge who had retired, his secretary became my secretary. This worked for a short time, but we soon parted ways. She was transferred to a position at the main courthouse, and we were both happy with the change.

Despite these many differences, the transition to the Labour Court was not difficult for me. The case law was different, but many of the issues and principles that underpinned it were the same. In a way, the work was less complex. We dealt with issues that took place within the province, which meant that we did not face constitutional challenges to the jurisdiction of the court as we had at the Canada Labour Relations Board. As well, I did not face the type of multi-party hearings that we frequently had at the board and that were very demanding to run. With the exception of complaints against unions for failing to represent employees in their grievances, the remainder of our work consisted of appeals from labour commissioners.

We only sat three days every two weeks. Some considered it to be a soft job. Rumour had it that working on our court was considered a "pre-retirement job." I did not find that to be the case. Though I was not sitting five days a week, my hours were spent hard at work. For instance, most of our work involved appeals from a lower tribunal. This meant listening to the hearings of the labour commissioners, which was a tedious and time-consuming process. I learned early on from my predecessor, the late Marc Brière, how to circumvent the lengthy listening ordeal. He usually asked the parties not only to specify the issue in appeal but also to specify, on the recording of the hearing, where the evidence of their allegations would be found. In that way, he did not have to spend many hours listening to irrelevant evidence but was instead able to immediately zone in on the essence of the debate. I followed his method and found it eased my workload considerably.

Another time-consuming aspect of our work, since we were a collegial court, was reading the judgments of our colleagues before they were sent to the parties and published. Although a judge could render a judgment even if one (or several) of the judge's colleagues disagreed with the decision, we attempted to reach consensus whenever we could. Our decisions provided guidelines and allowed lawyers and parties to have an idea of how the Labour Court would determine particular labour issues, so it was important that we were in agreement.

Early in my career, I heard that one of the judges at the Labour Court was upset about my appointment. Apparently, he had said: "We have many competent labour lawyers in Quebec. Why did we have to import an Anglophone from Ontario for a position on the Quebec Labour Court?" I knew the stakes for my first judgment would be high. After writing my first judgment, I anxiously awaited the reaction from my colleagues. Comments concerning our judgments were generally circulated to each other through our assistants. However, rather than send his comments to me via his assistant, this colleague came to my office and handed me the copy of my draft judgment on which he had written: "Excellent judgment." After congratulating me on my decision, he said he understood why I had been appointed as a judge on the court. I appreciated his comments and felt vindicated.

I was somewhat concerned, before I began to work at the Labour Court, about sitting alone. I was used to the hearings at the Canada Labour Relations Board where I presided over cases with two members. That provided me with the opportunity to discuss the evidence and consult the panel members about the decision to be rendered. I had grown used to the collaborative nature of those discussions. To my surprise, I found it was easier to sit alone than on a panel. I did not have to deal with differing opinions of the members on my panel or convince them to adopt the same position as I had.

I will always remember the one case at the Canada Labour Relations Board where I was presiding over a hearing and my two panel members came to a different conclusion than the one I had reached. Even though I was the vice-chair, and they were only members on the panel, every board decision was rendered by the majority. In that case, my decision became the dissenting decision on my own panel, which was rather embarrassing for me.

Unfortunately, my stay at the Quebec Labour Court was short. The court was abolished in 2004, after I had been there for only four years, and all of the judges who were not eligible for retirement were transferred to the Court of Quebec. I did not know when I took the position that the minister of labour had intended for some time to abolish our court and replace it with a labour commission, in line with the labour commissions and labour boards that existed in all the other Canadian provinces.

Fortunately, as I later learned, the minister of labour and the minister of justice were not communicating their plans with each other. The minister of justice was advised of the shortage of judges on the Quebec Labour Court and of the need to fill a vacancy. Unaware of the intention of the minister of labour to eliminate the Labour Court, the minister of justice had opened a position on the court and announced the vacancy. It was the position that I had obtained. If the two ministers had been in better communication, I would never have gotten my start in the Quebec judicial system. In that eventuality, who knows where my career might have taken me.

Instead, my transfer to the Court of Quebec took place, as planned, in the fall of 2004. I was given the choice of sitting in the Civil Division of the court, the Criminal Division, or in Youth Court. I immediately eliminated the possibility of transferring to the Criminal Division as I had never practised that area of the law and remembered very little from law school. In addition, I was made aware that most decisions in criminal cases were rendered from the bench. I was not certain that I would be able to issue a judgment, in French, immediately after hearing a case. I preferred taking time to review the case and write up my decision.

I decided to observe the proceedings at Youth Court for a couple of days. My husband had encouraged me to consider that division for my transfer since it was a specialized court, as was the Labour Court, and it was in a separate location from the other divisions. It would be more like the environment of the Labour Court than the Civil Division, which was in the main courthouse. He was probably right in that regard. However, after a very short period of time, I eliminated that possibility as well. I found the cases of the Youth Court emotionally draining. One of the cases I observed concerned a father who wanted to take his children to the Middle East; his ex-wife, who was the children's mother, was opposed. She was afraid that he would not return with the children. I had finished my observation period and was not present to hear how the case ended, but I was glad I did not have to make that decision.

I found it hard to understand how a judge could know what was in the best interest of the children, given our legal background. I wondered why we were empowered to make decisions concerning the fate of children who are abused or who need protection. While my views were not shared by my colleagues, it seemed to me that psychologists, psychiatric social workers, and special educators were more suited than judges to deal with such cases. In addition, I had never had children, and I was not convinced that I would be the best judge in cases affecting their well-being.

That left me with a sole remaining option: transferring to the Civil Division of the Court of Quebec.

Chapter 4

Off the Deep End and into the Court of Quebec

My transfer to the Civil Division of the Court of Quebec was traumatic. I was totally unprepared for the new nature of my work. Though I was still a judge, I was dealing with a totally different area of law, one that I had never practised as a lawyer. It took considerable time and effort to become familiar with the work I was assigned to do. That effort, on the other hand, led to a successful decades-long career.

All the provinces in Canada, except Quebec, operate under common law, which is based primarily on precedent. Although some laws are written; in most instances, the law is established by past decisions. This means that judgments that are rendered by a court are followed in succeeding cases unless the cases can be distinguished. The province of Quebec, on the other hand, has a mixed legal system consisting of both private law, which is governed by French civil law, and public law, which operates according to English common law. Public law sets the rules between the individual and society,[1] while private law concerns the relationship between persons. Private law is codified in the *Civil Code of Québec*.[2] This code contains a

Chapter 4

1 Public law includes constitutional law, administrative law, and criminal law.

2 *Civil Code of Québec*, CQLR c CCQ-1991.

comprehensive statement of rules governing such areas as birth, marriage, successions, property, contracts, liability, sales, leasing, donations, loans, insurance, employment, and so on.

While the civil law regime in Quebec is written, case law also plays a role. Lawsuits are decided on the basis of the written law, the evidence presented in court, and the precedent of previous judgments. Contrary to criminal law, where the Crown must prove its case beyond reasonable doubt, in civil law cases, the plaintiff must only prove the case by a preponderance of proof in order to succeed—that is, the plaintiff's version of the case must be more probable than that of the defendant.

Before a hearing commences, the judge receives a file outlining the facts and positions of both parties, the exhibits, and, in cases where experts are involved, their reports as well. At trial, the judge hears not only both parties but also the witnesses of each party. The judge obtains an explanation of the various exhibits and, where there are experts, hears the position and explanation of the expert witnesses. By the end of a trial, a story emerges. At times, witnesses contradict themselves. At other times, one witness contradicts another witness. Most often, the parties differ on some aspect of the case. Sometimes, the issue concerns a question of law, but, most often, the parties have different versions of the facts. I would sometimes wonder whether the two parties were even testifying about the same events.

THE ABSENCE OF A SCHOOL FOR JUDGES

In France, students who plan to be judges attend *l'École de la magistrature* (the school for judges). In Canada, no such school exists. Judges are named by the minister of justice from among practising lawyers and, in rare cases, from the ranks of politicians or law professors. A lawyer, when appointed, becomes a judge overnight, with all the trappings and responsibilities that go along with it. There is necessarily a change in perspective when someone moves from a career as a lawyer to that of a judge. Rather than defend the position of a client, a judge must consider both positions in the context of the law and render a fair, unbiased decision. However, lawyers who are appointed to the bench generally have a background in litigation. They are used to court proceedings, including the questioning of witnesses, carrying out cross examinations, raising objections, and presenting closing arguments.

That was certainly true in my case. I had litigated as a lawyer and even sat as a Labour Court judge. The problem was that I had little knowledge of civil law. It had been more than twenty years since I had graduated from law school, and I had not looked at my *Civil Code* or my *Code of Civil Procedure* again until this transfer.[3]

When my transfer took place, all of my colleagues on the Labour Court decided to take their retirement, leaving only one other member of that court and me to be transferred to the Court of Quebec. Neither of us had accumulated enough years as a judge to retire. I was given a few months to study the Quebec *Civil Code* and the *Code of Civil Procedure*, but I fell into an administrative black hole and received very little help from my assigned mentor. I spent that time reading the codes but without any guidance. I had been left to my own resources and was not happy about my changed circumstances.

3 *Code of Civil Procedure*, CQLR c C-25 (now the *New Code of Civil Procedure*, CQLR c C-25.01).

While I had been given an observation period, watching a few trials for a couple of days, it was not very meaningful. I quickly ascertained that I lacked the necessary background to fully understand the proceedings. My colleagues spent little time discussing the cases after the hearings, and I never saw the judgments that had been written to see the outcome of the trials. My few days of observation were far from sufficient for what lay ahead. However, even though I did not feel ready, it was time for me to take my place on the bench.

THE CHALLENGES OF MY FIRST TRIAL IN CIVIL LAW

My first day on the bench in the Civil Division of the Court of Quebec finally arrived on 21 February 2005. It was, needless to say, rather traumatic! I put on my long black robe, which has a red stripe on each side of the front panel. I placed the white bib around my neck and checked my appearance in the mirror. For my colleagues, the sole difference in their dress when transitioning to a judge was the red stripe on each side of their new robes, which would identify them as judges and distinguish them from the lawyers. I, on the other hand, felt as if I was going to a costume party: neither the lawyers nor the judges in the Labour Court wore robes. Of course, I kept such thoughts to myself.

The first thing I did was collect my files for that day's hearing, but my bailiff quickly took them from me. In the Court of Quebec, as in the Superior Court and the Court of Appeal, judges do not carry their own files or even law books. Having a bailiff carry one's *Civil Code*, *Code of Civil Procedure*, and files is a carryover from a long-standing tradition in the courts, as are our robes.

My assistant, Josette, who was also my court clerk, entered the courtroom before I did and noted the presence of the parties. Josette, who I had hired at the Quebec Labour Court and who followed me to the Court of Quebec, was essential in helping to run a smooth hearing. I stood waiting in the corridor outside the courtrooms, which is restricted to judges and their staff. When Josette finished her task, the bailiff rang a buzzer and announced my presence, asking everyone to rise and turn off their cellular devices. I walked up the few steps to my chair, which was behind a small desk and higher than the other seats in the courtroom. I was thankful that no one could see the butterflies in my stomach.

I had been told by my coordinator that he had selected a relatively simple file for my first case. I was not convinced since there were three parties involved in the lawsuit rather than the usual two adversaries.

The case concerned hidden defects in a newly purchased property. The plaintiff had bought a house and, shortly after, found water seeping into the property from the roof and into the basement, which had completely flooded. She sued both the seller and the building inspector for the cost of her repairs as well as for her damages, her troubles, and inconvenience. The outset of the case was uneventful. The lawyers for each party identified themselves and stated that they were ready to proceed. The lawyers, in turn, presented a brief summary of their clients' positions. However, before presenting the witnesses, the lawyer for one of the defendants stood up and announced: "I oppose the production of the plaintiff's exhibits, since the plaintiff did not file a 403."[4] My stress

4 The number referred to a section in the *Code of Civil Procedure* (now the *New Code of Civil Procedure*, s 264), which states that a party can

level soared. I had no idea what she was referring to. A 403 sounded like the number of a highway, which clearly was not what the lawyer was referring to. Rather than appear ignorant, I suggested that we deal with her objection at the appropriate time and asked the lawyer for the plaintiff if he was ready to proceed.

The first witness was presented as an expert. After presenting his qualifications, the opposing party has the right to question the witness's education, background, and experience in an attempt to disqualify the individual as an expert. It is rare that the qualifications of an expert are challenged, and I had no doubt that, after the questioning, I would be able to declare this witness as an expert in his field. To my surprise, the lawyer for one of the defendants raised an objection. She informed me that the witness was under investigation by his professional association and claimed that he no longer had the standing to testify as an expert. Unable to make a ruling, I adjourned the court proceedings for a brief period so that I could verify the validity of the objection.

I went back to my office and quickly tried to determine how to handle the issue. There was no time for extensive research. In fact, there was little time for any research. I could not spend several hours in my office trying to determine the answer. I called another judge who was not sitting that day and asked for help. My colleague asked whether the complaint had been heard and whether a decision had been rendered by the professional association concerned. If not, he advised me, there was no reason not to hear the witness as an expert. I thanked my

---

call on the opposite party, by means of a written notice, to admit to the integrity of the information that a document contains.

colleague profusely and returned to the courtroom, feeling even more anxious than when I began earlier in the morning. The hearing proceeded. No disciplinary decision had been rendered in the case of this witness, so I allowed him to testify.

This was not the only objection that the lawyers raised that day. There were many more. One of the two defendants claimed that the action could not be maintained against him based on a technicality. I took this objection *sous réserve*—that is, under advisement, which meant that my decision on the objection would not be rendered immediately but only when I wrote my judgment. As other objections were raised, I handled some in the moment, but most I took under advisement.

I felt as if the day would never end. This was supposed to be a simple case, but each of the three parties was pointing their finger at the other two. There were regular witnesses, three expert witnesses, expert reports, and numerous exhibits dealing with subject matter about which I had no knowledge. Four-thirty finally arrived. It was the end of the hearing day. The case was scheduled for three days—little did I know that it would take eight days to hear the entire case. That first day, I remained in my office long enough to begin typing the essential facts of the day's hearing, then hurried home. I got through the door and burst into tears.

This is not the typical first day of hearing of any new judge. Judges are usually appointed in the field of law in which they have practised. For the most part, they have pleaded the same type of cases that they hear and decide as a judge. They are familiar with the law involved and with the court proceedings. My situation was most unusual and not one that I would want anyone else to experience.

In retrospect, it seemed to me that the government had concluded that, since the judges from the Labour Court had a law degree and had sat as judges for several years, it did not matter what court we sat on. However, our transfer to an entirely different court, with a different set of laws, was akin to taking a doctor who had only practised psychiatry and suddenly requiring him to perform open heart surgery, without any further training. I quickly learned to adapt. Judges who have a civil law background generally begin their analysis of a file by referring to the provisions of the *Civil Code of Québec* covering the subject matter involved in the case. Since I did not remember the civil law that I had learned in law school when I first began sitting in the Civil Division of the court, my starting point was listening to the evidence and trying to figure out what made sense and what was a just outcome for the case.

Such an approach could be considered as heretical, but the law is supposed to have a common-sense basis. More often than not, after consulting a lawyer in our legal services or one of my colleagues, I learned that my conclusion about a case, based on good common sense and fairness, was the same as the conclusion that would be reached if the case was approached from a legal point of view by applying the *Civil Code*. Over time, I learned to trust my instincts and to balance my common-sense reasoning with civil law and case law in all of my judgments.

THE CHALLENGE OF TECHNOLOGY

Dealing with civil law was not my only challenge. Another challenge I was faced with was the use of technology. When I first entered my new office, there was a large computer on my desk. Although smartphones and iPads were in common use, I had never used a computer before. My assistant asked me whether I wanted her to give me my password, and I told her that it could wait. She asked again the following day, and I responded with the same answer.

This exchange continued for a few days until my assistant, who was astute enough to understand the situation and did not want to embarrass me, advised me that there was an information technology department and that one of the technicians was available to meet with me. She arranged for a meeting, and I was given a crash course on how to use my new computer.

THE CHALLENGE OF DEALING WITH OBJECTIONS

A further challenge was dealing with objections. The law involves many rules governing evidence. When one party attempts to introduce evidence that is inadmissible in law, the lawyer for the opposing party will usually rise and say: "Objection." With few exceptions, the judge does not rule on the objection immediately without allowing for argument. The lawyer who is objecting must state the grounds of his objection and, if the lawyer has not done so, the judge asks him for the basis of his position. Following the lawyer's explanation, the opposite party—namely, the party who is seeking to present the evidence, has the right to respond. On occasion, there is also an opportunity for the objecting party to provide further arguments. The judge then renders a decision on the objection.

A well-known example is that of hearsay. A witness cannot relate what someone else (a third party) has said since it is not possible to cross-examine the third party. If a witness says: "My aunt told me her walls are red," it does not prove that the walls are actually painted red; the testimony is not admissible to prove the colour of her walls.

There are numerous objections for different situations. There are also numerous exceptions to the rules. The list is extremely long and includes objections based on the lack of relevance of the evidence, the production of a copy and not the original of a document, the attempt to contradict the terms of a written document by means of testimony, the confidential nature of the communication between a lawyer and his client, and so on. One of the well-known textbooks on the subject of objections runs close to two thousand pages.[5]

In labour law, the rules about evidence were far more relaxed. For example, hearsay evidence was not automatically rejected, copies without the originals could be admitted into evidence, and testimony to establish the facts of a case was less restricted.

Although I had learned the rules of evidence in law school, I had forgotten most of them—it had simply been too many years since I was a student. When I began sitting, I was far from certain how to rule on any objection except the most basic ones. As I already indicated, I decided that, whenever possible, if I was not sure, I would take the objection under advisement, without rendering a decision on the objection right away. I allowed the evidence to be presented, and then when I drafted my judgment, I decided if the evidence should be admitted or not. I thought this would enable me to easily deal with the problem of objections, which were raised in virtually every trial. Unfortunately, I was wrong!

---

5 Donald Béchard, *Manuel de l'Objection*, 3d ed (Cowansville, QC: Éditions Yvon Blais, 2009). This was the edition that I used when I was on the bench. A fourth edition was released in 2019.

At one of my first hearings, I had accumulated close to twenty-five objections, all of which I had taken "under advisement" or "under reserve." Initially, I thought I could simply admit or reject the evidence without indicating the reason for doing so, or I could even avoid dealing with the objection altogether. I mentioned this to one of my colleagues who looked rather shocked. She pointed out that it would take considerable work dealing with each objection when I drafted my judgment. She informed me, to my dismay, that if I failed to discuss how I decided each of the objections, it would constitute grounds for appeal.

I raised the subject with another of my colleagues, who was an expert on evidence, and asked him for his advice. He suggested that, just before the parties were to begin presenting their arguments, I should ask them to reiterate any objections they had made during the trial concerning the evidence and the grounds that supported their position, if they still wanted the court to deal with their objections. If they did not raise the objections again, I did not have to analyze and rule on them. His suggestion was a godsend. It made my life on the bench considerably less stressful until I was more knowledgeable in this area of legal evidence.

There is one exception to waiting to rule on objections—that is, the case of confidential communication between a lawyer and a client, which covers consultations, discussions, opinions, documents, and the like. They all remain confidential and cannot be divulged unless the client chooses to do so since the privilege belongs to the client and not to the lawyer.

In one of my cases, a client sued his lawyer, claiming that the lawyer had unlawfully taken money from his trust account that was owed to the client. The client wanted an accounting of the money and the reimbursement of the funds owed to him. The lawyer objected to revealing the information, claiming that the information sought regarding his law firm's trust account was subject to solicitor-client privilege. The client maintained that the information he sought was important in order to establish the lawyer's responsibility and was not privileged information. Clearly, the issue was important for both parties.

I listened to each party's position and had no idea whether a trust account benefited from the privilege of confidentiality since it was not a usual objection. But what I did know was that I could not allow the evidence if, in fact, it was privileged information. My usual escape route of stating that the objection was taken under advisement and then deciding the outcome of the objection when I drafted my judgment would not work here. I needed time to analyze the case law and more than a ten-minute break in the hearing. I decided to adjourn and asked the parties to present their positions in writing, which gave me the time to consider their arguments and review the case law. I ultimately dismissed the objection, concluding that the lawyer could not hide behind an argument of solicitor-client privilege and refuse to transmit the requested information.

Over the course of my time on the bench, I was more readily able to deal with the objections concerning civil evidence, but I was thankful that I did not have another case where I had to suspend the hearing. I realized that some objections were simply grandstanding on the part of lawyers. I admonished a particular lawyer for objecting to the evidence to such an extent that he was disruptive, and I was unable to hear the case. I warned him that if his objections were not truly sound, I would not entertain any further ones.

I also realized that lawyers want a ruling on their objections immediately, if possible, irrespective of how I ruled on those objections. When a lawyer objects to a question that the opposing lawyer asks a witness and the judge upholds the objection, the question is not permitted. In such cases, the opposing lawyer will move on to his next question. In one instance, I said: "It is rejected."[6] I was referring to the objection, dismissing it. This meant that the question was allowed and that the witness would answer it. However, the opposing lawyer misunderstood my ruling and thought that I was not allowing his question. Surprisingly, the lawyer did not appear visibly upset. He proceeded to ask the witness the next question, without skipping a beat.

REFUSING FILES

As I became more comfortable with presiding over civil lawsuits, there remained one exception. Tax was never my forte in law school. I found the subject matter so difficult that I dropped my tax course early in the first semester of my last year and switched to a course on labour law. However, tax law was one of the subjects tested on bar school exams, and to be admitted to the Quebec bar, I had to pass every exam. I was more than nervous about having to write an exam in that area of law, but, thankfully for me, the exam was comprised of both tax law and labour law. I failed the portion on tax but excelled in labour law, which gave me an overall passing grade.

6 "It is rejected" is a literal translation from French. In English, a judge would say "over-ruled."

Needless to say, I was terrified of presiding over a tax file. I hoped that I would never have to deal with a tax issue, but, I was alarmed to learn that judges on the Court of Quebec do deal with such cases. Eventually, a case involving an appeal of a decision of the minister of revenue of Quebec was assigned to me.

The appellant contested the minister's decision to refuse an interest payment deduction that resulted in increasing the appellant's taxable revenue. He also contested the decision that refused a deduction he had claimed for a business investment loss. After hearing the evidence, I reviewed several judgments dealing with similar issues. I spent several days studying the legislation and jurisprudence since I was not at all familiar with this area of the law. I struggled with the notions, but I was finally able to write a judgment that I felt confident about. After I had completed the judgment, I mentioned the facts of the case to my husband. He immediately said: "You're absolutely right, the case should be dismissed. He can't deduct his interest payments since his loan was not incurred for the purpose of gaining income." Bjørn added that, from the facts I had mentioned, the appellant also should not obtain a deduction for a business investment loss.

I was incredibly frustrated. I had spent days working on the case. Meanwhile, my husband, who has a master's degree in business administration and prepares our tax returns, would have been able to render a decision from the bench. On the other hand, I was pleased to know that I had rendered a judgment that was correct.

At a dinner party, sometime after presiding over another tax case that gave me as much trouble as the first, a judge who sat on the Superior Court was unabashed to admit that she refused to hear any construction cases. I was taken aback and asked how she managed to avoid presiding over those cases. She replied that she had told her coordinator that she would not hear any files dealing with construction. When any were assigned to her, she simply returned them to her coordinator.

The next time I received a tax file, I promptly went to my coordinator's office and told him that I would not accept the case. I said I was not shirking my responsibilities and that I would accept any other file in its place. My coordinator appeared startled. "It's really more of a civil law case," he said. I disputed his qualification of the file. "I find tax law incomprehensible, and I cannot render a sound and fair judgment on this case," I insisted. I left his office, wondering what would happen next. There were no dire consequences. Another file, one involving a claim for damages, arrived at my office the following day. I was never assigned another tax case again.

Chapter 5

My Life as a Judge in Court

The Court of Quebec was very different from the previous tribunals where I had sat. It was particularly distinct from the small Labour Court where, even on my first day, I was like a fish "in" water. Instead of a dozen judges specialized in one area of the law and situated only in Montreal and Quebec City, we numbered slightly over three hundred judges, hearing various types of cases, and we sat throughout the province. Everything was different—from where our officers were situated to the way in which we engaged with others at court, the kinds of cases we heard, the volume of work, our support staff, and even the administration of the court.

JUDGES' OFFICES

The Court of Quebec in Montreal, located in the massive main courthouse in Old Montreal, is a large building with seventeen floors. It houses the judges of the Court of Quebec and its associated tribunals, such as the Human Rights Tribunal, as well as the judges of the Superior Court. The offices of the judges are in a section that is completely closed to the public. In addition to the judges' offices and the courtrooms, there is a registry office, a well-stocked library, a cafeteria, a judges' dining room, offices of administrative staff, and cells where the accused wait prior to attending their court hearing. There is even a marriage celebration room.

The Court of Quebec has a layer of administration that, coming from the Labour Court, I was not used to. Not only was there a chief justice, but there were also associate chief justices, coordinating judges, and associate coordinating judges, a legal department, an information technology department, and an administration team that oversaw the many secretaries, clerks, and bailiffs. In addition, there were constables assigned to the courthouse.

Since I was used to going to the office of my chief justice at the Labour Court and knocking on his door when I wished to discuss any matter, I initially approached my chief justice at the Court of Quebec in the same way. When I arrived at the door leading to his office, I was faced with two secretaries who noted that I did not have an appointment and wanted to know why I was there. They were rather surprised and perplexed by my presence. It was apparently most uncommon for a judge to show up at the office of the head of the court, particularly when a visit was not slotted. I learned that, to see the chief justice, I needed to make an appointment and state the purpose of my visit.

Our offices were also different from those in the Labour Court. Each one was very spacious, with large windows and a view over either Old Montreal or the city's port. Two judges were paired in each office; their assistants had their desks in the centre room, while the judges' chambers were on either side. Best of all, each office had a private bathroom.

Initially, all the offices had the same furniture: a large wood desk that filled a good part of the room, a floor-to-ceiling bookcase, filing cabinets that covered an entire wall, and a sofa, which was essentially a covered bench in a nondescript colour that was anchored to the wall. We were given a relatively modest budget to change the furniture. I clearly could not purchase a modern leather couch, stylish leather chairs, and other items to turn my office into the chic environment I would have liked to have. I needed an interior decorator.

My assistant Josette recommended a woman who she had used. Michèle Belair Pagnettit turned out to be an excellent designer—rather costly but very effective. She immediately understood my taste, what I wanted, and the constraints I had, given the modest court budget. She brought me to a wholesaler where I was able to purchase some modern black chairs in inexpensive leather. Then, with her help, I had my sofa recovered in a beautiful grey material. Although the sofa was still anchored to the wall, it looked rather attractive. She suggested re-staining the bookshelves a rich dark brown-black colour and having the walls repainted in a creamy beige tone. These modifications were modest in cost and fell within my budget.

After the renovations took place, I brought approximately fifteen pieces of artwork from my home and hung them in my office, in the interior corridor, and even in the toilet area. It looked like an art gallery. Despite my shoestring budget, I managed to give my office a fresh and smart look. I found the space so appealing and welcoming, and Michèle, my designer, was so helpful that I hired her many years later to assist me in renovating a new home.

This renovation helped me feel anchored in my new space. In the previous few weeks, I had undergone several office changes, some that were welcome while others that were not. My first office flooded when a toilet on the floor above me leaked through the ceiling. I was moved to another office, with my assistant, while the repairs were taking place. I was told the move would be temporary, but it turned out to be rather lengthy. It was not only a small office with old furniture, but it was incredibly inconvenient since it was relatively far from the courtroom in which I heard my cases. Then I learned that a number of offices were vacant, having been newly renovated. I requested one of them, and my request was accepted. I moved into my third office in a short space of time. I assumed it was the last, and it was then that I hired my designer, Michèle, and settled in.

Sometime later, another office was vacated, and I was asked to move. However, since I now had new carpets, newly painted walls in a pleasing colour that I had chosen, and refinished bookcases, I wanted to remain in my office. I strongly objected to the proposed move. I successfully pointed to my seniority and ultimately stayed where I was, very close to my courtroom. A more junior colleague took the available office.

RELATIONS AT THE COURT

Judges have little or no say in the choice of their offices, and it is the same when it comes to who becomes a colleague in their court. While members in private clubs choose new members with whom they would like to associate, spend time, and share mutually enjoyed activities, this is not the case in a court. New judges are chosen by the minister of justice, and current judges are not consulted. As a result, there are affinities among certain judges and not among others. When I was there, some of the judges were relatively solitary and mixed little with other judges, while others formed cliques and social groups both small and large.

As mentioned earlier, judges' offices are paired such that their assistants work in a central room with the offices of the two paired judges on either side. Relations between the two judges were most often cordial. However, there were occasions when a judge moved his office. It was only through the court rumour mill that we learned whether the change stemmed from a rift in the relationship between the two judges or whether it was their assistants who did not get along. The only moves that were not questioned were those involving a promotion to the position of coordinator or to a higher position in the court hierarchy.

When I arrived at the Court of Quebec, I noted that the male judges tended to stick together. They got together for lunch and discussions and left the courthouse in small groups to eat meals in various nearby restaurants or in the judges' dining room, which is a large comfortable area, closed to the public, with full course lunches served at a reasonable price, but without wine. The woman judges were not technically excluded, but few joined the men. As the years passed, a greater number of women were named to the court, and the "old boys' network" changed. There were fewer cliques and more mixing between the male and female judges. At times, occasionally during the day but most often after hours, several judges would congregate in the office of one of the well-liked female judges and discuss cases, seek advice from colleagues, or simply chat about their day.

Contrary to some company policies, there was no prohibition against having a relationship with another judge or staff member. While it was not common, I did see a number of relationships form between judges or between judges and staff. In a few cases, the couples even married. This is not surprising. Relationships often develop in universities, hospitals, offices, companies, and other organizations. The court, in this respect, was no different.

WHAT TYPE OF JUDGE ARE YOU?

During the time I was on the bench, I was constantly asked: "What type of judge are you?" "A good one," I would say when I was being flippant. Then I would provide a proper answer, indicating the type of cases I heard in court (since this was clearly what the person was asking about). I explained that I sat as a judge in a civil court and heard civil and commercial law cases. I quickly learned that this meant nothing to a layperson. So, I changed my answer and listed the nature of the civil or commercial cases that I decided, such as civil responsibility claims, consumer protection claims, bills of exchange, breach of contract, latent defects, and so on. Again, my legalese most often meant nothing to the person asking the question.

I learned to present my explanations in such a way that everyone could understand the nature of the cases I heard and decided. Typical of the examples I provided were the following subjects:

- A lawyer, accountant, or other professional sues for his fees that have not been paid.
- One party sues another for prematurely ending a contract.
- A buyer of a house sues the seller because of hidden problems in the property.
- An insured person sues his insurance company that refuses to pay for a claim.
- A patient sues his doctor or his dentist for malpractice.
- A client sues his contractor for work he claims was poorly done or left unfinished.

- An employee sues his employer for what he considers to be a wrongful dismissal.
- An individual sues a store for defective merchandise he purchased.
- A client sues a service provider for failing to provide the service offered.
- A person sues another for a loan he provided that was not repaid.

The list can go on and on. The defendant, namely the person or the company that is sued, usually presents a defence, and the defences are very typical. Most often, after reading the lawsuit, the nature of the defence is exactly what I would expect. For example:

- The defendant refuses to pay professional fees because the defendant was dissatisfied with the services provided.
- The defendant ends a contract and refuses to pay the remaining amount owed because of a claim the work was badly done.
- The defendant does not repay the money received from the plaintiff because the defendant claims it was a gift and not a loan.
- The seller of a house defends against a claim, alleging that the defects were apparent and not hidden.
- The insurer denies payment to the insured because of the insured's failure to disclose a material or essential fact.
- The company that is sued for unjust dismissal alleges the employee's dismissal is justified because the employee performed badly, and so on.

Of course, I never gave such a long list of examples when asked about my work. However, I did find that an explanation with some examples was both necessary and satisfactory. Most people only think of criminal trials or divorce cases when they think about court cases. Once I gave an explanation, the puzzled looks that I saw when I said I handled cases in civil and commercial law would disappear.

LEMONS

Some cases that we heard were common, while others were not. While at the Court of Quebec, I heard many cases concerning used cars that were purchased from dealers but were not fit for the road. In most of these cases, the purchasers wanted to annul the sale and get their money back. In other cases, they wanted to keep the vehicles but wanted the dealer to pay for the necessary repairs to make the car driveable. Typically, the cars that were involved were older used cars and the purchaser had not paid very much money for them. As well, as a general rule in such cases, the dealer would assure the buyer that the car had been inspected and was in good working order. However, this was rarely true.

In one case, at the time of purchase, the dealer claimed that the vehicle the young woman wanted to buy had been verified at his garage and ran well. Because of this, he refused to allow her to have the car examined elsewhere. The woman, reassured by the dealer's claim, bought the car. She immediately began to have problems. She could not drive more than fifty kilometres an hour, and the transmission was defective. After bringing the car back to the dealer for repair, he assured her that the problem was fixed. Instead, as soon as she drove on a highway, a red light came up on her dashboard and smoke started billowing out of the hood. When she returned to the dealer, she was told that the radiator pipe was cut and needed to be changed. After this second repair, the car was stalling, and the woman found that changing gears was difficult.

She no longer had any confidence in having another repair carried out by the dealer and brought it to a garage instead. She was told that the cost of the required repairs would amount to more than what she had paid for the car at the outset. She returned the car to the dealer and instituted a lawsuit against him, claiming the reimbursement of the price of the car as well as various costs incurred because of the breakdowns. The dealer stated that it was not a new car and that there are always repairs to be done. In any event, he maintained there was no guarantee for that vehicle.

Quebec is generally very protective of consumers. Cars that are over five years old, with more than eighty thousand kilometres, are not covered by the guarantees foreseen for vehicles in the *Consumer Protection Act*.[1] However, the Act has a general guarantee that states that goods that are the object of a contract must last for a reasonable period of time.

Here, the purchaser had bought a car that had problems from the very moment that she drove out of the dealer's premises, and they persisted even after continued repairs. During the month after her purchase, she only had the car for a few days. After that, the car remained at the dealer for repairs. In short, she was unable to enjoy the car she had bought for any reasonable period of time and could not use it as a means of transportation. Our case

---

Chapter 5

1 *Consumer Protection Act*, CQLR c P-40.1.

law has concluded that, if merchandise does not last for a reasonable period of time after it has been purchased, the vendor is presumed to have sold a product that was not in good condition. Given the evidence, it was not difficult to grant the buyer the reimbursement of the money that she had paid for the car she had purchased. It clearly was a "lemon."

RAT POISON AND OTHER EXHIBITS

In every case, parties must present evidence to support their claim or their defence. The evidence that a party brings to court consists of the party's testimony, the testimony of ordinary witnesses, the testimony of expert witnesses if there are any, and exhibits related to the case. When we refer to exhibits, most people think of documents, such as written contracts, deeds of sale, invoices, receipts, emails, and other items. However, an exhibit does not have to be a document. It can be any object.

At times, one of the parties may raise an objection to the submission of an exhibit presented by the opposing party to substantiate their position. After hearing from the parties, the judge then decides whether or not the document or object is admissible.

Examples of unacceptable exhibits have included estimates for repairs that do not identify the person or business providing the estimate, documents that are not signed (unless it meets other conditions, such as those used in the ordinary course of a business), and documents that are undated. Documents presented in a foreign language without any translation are also rejected. In other situations, valid objections concern the authenticity of a recording, a copy of a document rather than the original, and a document that has no pertinence to the litigation. Privileged communication, such as documents prepared by a lawyer for a client that contain the strategy for upcoming litigation, are also considered inadmissible. There are many reasons for refusing to admit an exhibit into evidence.

However, when exhibits were admissible and accepted into evidence, I advised the parties that they could retrieve their exhibits once the judgment in their case was rendered. Until the time the decision was transmitted to the parties, I kept the exhibits of each case in my office. That way, I could examine them if I needed to see them again. Emails and text messages are admissible, but, if they are not printed, then the party or the witness who wanted to produce them had to leave their smart phone with me. In one case, after I had finished my judgment, and it was issued, I was surprised to learn that the party who had remitted his iPhone as evidence in court had not retrieved it. It was only after my assistant called him several times that he returned to obtain his phone.

At any given time, I had a collection of exhibits in my office. They included badly stitched clothing, yarmulkes, a plank of warped wood that had been installed in a home, tubing used for plumbing, screws in different sizes, various parts of cars, a logbook, brochures of vacation sites, videos, and, very often, photographs of botched construction work. In one case, the purchaser of a home found an open box of rat poison in the basement when she moved in. She produced the box in court to establish that the seller knew the property was infested with rodents. She maintained that there would not have been a need to have that box of poison if the seller had not seen any rats. Josette, my assistant, wanted me to throw out the box. I refused to trash an exhibit. Josette refused to touch the box. I was anxious to finish that judgment as soon as possible. While I assumed that the purchaser did not want to come back to court to pick up the box of poison, we nevertheless contacted her since parties have the right to retrieve their exhibits. She did not return to claim the box of poison. After a couple of weeks, I finally told Josette that she could discard the box.

CONFLICT OF INTEREST

Judges are expected to be completely neutral and impartial in making their decisions. If a judge does not feel comfortable or able to decide in an impartial way, then he should recuse himself—that is, remove himself as a judge in a particular case.[2] This is done in the case of a lack of impartiality with respect to one or both of the parties or because of a conflict of interest. This can take place when a friend or family member appears in front of a judge, when there is a relationship with one of the parties, or when a conflict of interest exists such that the judge could feel obliged to rule in a particular manner. A financial relationship between a judge and one of the parties is also considered to constitute a conflict of interest, particularly when monies owed, by either one, are outstanding. The same principle applies when a judge has any preconceived ideas about the question in dispute.

The issue is not complicated when a conflict of interest involves a friend or relative. One day, a lawyer entered the

---

2 Bryan A Garner, ed, *Black's Law Dictionary*, 7th ed (St Paul, MN: West Group, 1999). The subject of recusation is dealt with in the *Code of Civil Procedure*, CQLR c C-25, ss 234ff. In the new *Code of Civil Procedure*, CQLR c C-25.01, situations where judges should recuse themselves are foreseen in s 202.

courtroom, took a look at me sitting on the bench, and asked my assistant whether there were other judges available to hear his motion. Josette, who as my court clerk sat in front of me, scribbled something on a piece of paper, then turned around and handed it to me. A question mark "?" was written on the note. I wrote back: "I know him; he is a good friend of mine. I can't hear his case."

Judges are also not supposed to hear cases where their former law firm is involved in the case unless a significant period of time has elapsed since they left practising law at that firm. After the Quebec Labour Court closed, there were outstanding cases that remained and needed to be heard. One of the last cases dealt with a complaint by a union member against his union for not representing him when he lost his job. Since I had previously sat on the Quebec Labour Court, the case was assigned to me.

I immediately noticed that the firm of Trudel Nadeau, the firm where I had practised during most of my career, was representing the union. One of the partners, who was an ex-colleague of mine, was acting on behalf of the union. I asked that the case be assigned to someone else, but my request was denied; there was no one else at the Court of Quebec who had a labour law background and was familiar with the issues involved in the case or with the case law involved.

I must admit that I found it amusing to have the senior attorney of the law firm where I had worked, and whom I knew well, rise when I entered the courtroom. However, parties are required to rise when the judge enters the courtroom. It is a rule governing behaviour in court and is considered as courtroom decorum. It signifies respect for the justice system and the court process rather than as a sign of deference for the particular judge hearing the case.

I was not very comfortable hearing the case. It was not only because my ex-partner was involved. I was also reluctant to hear the case since the employee who was complaining about his union's failure to represent him was a police officer, and my previous long-term significant other had been a police officer. In some ways, however, that made my position easier. Since there was reason for me to react favourably to both parties, I could not be accused of being partial to one over the other. I did hear the case, as required, and concentrated on the facts. Nevertheless, I was happy when the case ended.

RENDERING JUDGMENTS

Judgments can be provided to the parties verbally at the end of a hearing, or they can be sent in writing after the hearing is over. Many of my colleagues were able to render their judgments from the bench immediately after a case was heard. I never felt comfortable delivering my judgments that way, with the exception of uncontested cases and cases involving an order to confine an individual to a health institution, where we had to make the decision without delay. I wanted to be sure that I was satisfied with my decision on the outcome of a case and that I would not regret it afterwards. Although there were times when I struggled before reaching a conclusion, once my decision was written and issued, I did not look back and wish I had written a different one.

Since I rarely rendered judgments from the bench, I had to draft judgments in virtually all of the cases I heard. I was envious of the skill of my colleagues who could decide quickly and who could also quickly organize their thoughts and deliver a judgment in court at the end of a trial. Not only did they not have a judgment to write, but they could also use the time that was allotted to draft that case to work on other cases that required more time. When I first started at the Court of Quebec, I expected that I would eventually be able to emulate my colleagues. Unfortunately, that never happened. On the other hand, I hoped that the parties I presided over preferred to receive a written decision rather than an oral one and appreciated the opportunity to read my judgment on paper, where they could easily follow my reasoning.

I usually wrote easily. However, at times, I began writing a judgment and found that I hit a dead end. The facts were laid out in a coherent manner and the law was described, but when I attempted to write out the conclusion I had decided upon, the argument simply did not work. The writing felt tortured, and the analysis of the facts did not lead to the conclusion I was attempting to reach. When this happened, I stopped writing, reread my notes, and reconsidered the case. I tried to write a judgment based on the position of the opposing party. When the writing flowed easily, and the parts fell into place, I knew that this was the proper outcome. This was the advice I had received from my colleague, Richard Hornung, at the Canada Labour Relations Board. He advised me to reconsider my initial position when it became too difficult to justify a particular conclusion in a case.

We had six months from the time a hearing ended to issue our judgments. For cases heard in our Small Claims Court, the delay was four months. The Court of Quebec had an excellent schedule: one week on the bench, followed by one week for our deliberations ("la déliberé")—the period in which we could review our notes, read case law, reflect, reach a decision, and draft the judgment. Basically, for every day we sat, we were provided with one day to write. However, depending on what transpired during a hearing week, it was possible to have presided over a dozen or more cases. Unless a judge was able to render judgments from the bench, it was often difficult to draft judgments in all the cases we heard during a hearing week in our so called "writing week." It was much easier to write one judgment for a case that had lasted for five days than it was to write a number of judgments after we had heard several cases in the same week.

I tried to keep up to date and not have a backlog, and, for the most part, I succeeded. But, to do so, I began drafting the facts of a case as soon as I left the courtroom when the testimony, objections, and pleadings were fresh in my mind.

Contrary to the Superior Court, our cases were not continuous. If a case was scheduled for three days, and it was not finished at the end of that time, it was rescheduled. Often, the new date was set for a couple of months later. I almost never listened to the recording of the initial hearing. That was too time-consuming. My notes of the hearing, which I typed before the postponement, were the basis of my draft judgment and were extremely useful in recalling the evidence that I had heard earlier. Most often, I did not even need to reread the notes I had taken in the courtroom. My draft judgment was sufficient.

I often worked late at the office and continued to work even in the evenings when I was at home. Because I started writing right away at the end of each day in court, I managed to draft my judgments in a timely way. I never worked during my six-week summer vacation, and I even accumulated time off by handling extra work so that I could take a holiday during the winter months. Not so for many of my colleagues. Most of the other judges did not work as hard as I did during the judicial year, and, as a result, many of them suffered at holiday time. They were behind in their writing and had accumulated so many judgments to write that they had to work during their vacation. In fact, often a good part of their summer vacation was spent drafting their decisions. No one wanted to get a letter from the chief justice, reminding them that they were approaching the judicial deadline for issuing their judgment.

During my week of deliberations, I worked at home where I had fewer distractions than at the courthouse. While I was drafting my judgments, I took short breaks during the day to get chores done rather than taking an extended lunch period to go out for a meal. I quickly realized that my dry cleaner, dressmaker, and other service personnel who I saw during my breaks thought it was my day off or that I was on vacation. I had to explain that I was working from home that week and doing errands during my lunch break.

I recall reading an article in a newspaper many years ago that was accompanied by a photograph of a judge who was mowing his lawn during the day. The reporter supposed that judges did not work very hard; he wrote that they had a "soft job." I was angry when I read the article, knowing that most judges are conscientious; they take their work seriously and work very hard. What the reporter did not know (or care to find out!) was whether that particular judge was truly not working or simply taking a break from drafting a difficult judgment.

It is true that the number of hours spent in the courtroom is not overly onerous, which often gives the public the impression that judges do not work very hard. However, the reality is that the time spent in the courtroom is only a small part of the time worked. Reading case law, reviewing the law and the facts of the case, thinking about how to resolve the conflicting positions of the parties, reaching a conclusion, and finally writing the actual judgment take up a prodigious amount of time.

I did not decide easily. The law itself was usually the least difficult aspect for me to establish. More problematic was the conflicting versions presented by the parties involved and the credibility of the witnesses. For me, writing was the easy part. This was not the case for other colleagues. Some of my colleagues decided quickly but had difficulty putting the facts of the case they had heard into a comprehensible story. Sometimes, I wished that we could work in teams consisting of those who decided easily and those who wrote easily. But that was never the case.

Chapter 6

Important Cases, Lawyers, and Litigants

Over the course of an average hearing week, a judge hears approximately a dozen lawsuits. I heard eight to ten cases in Small Claims Court on Mondays and Tuesdays, then one or more contested cases over the next three days, in addition to a number of uncontested cases. Most of these lawsuits are not newsworthy and do not serve as a precedent.

There are, however, judgments that make an impact. These judgments might be quoted or followed by another judge or even written up in the newspapers. It was always a source of pride for me when one of my judgments made such an impact, and it happened several times over the course of my long career. The cases described in this chapter are some of my most unusual ones as well as those I heard that were particularly out of the ordinary. I also detail the characters (whether that be a lawyer, a defendant, or a plaintiff) who made my life interesting day in and day out.

SETTING PRECEDENT

In construction cases, employers are required to respect certain safety standards and assure that their employees are not subject to dangerous conditions at their worksites.

If, by any action or omission, an employer does anything that will directly and seriously compromise the health, safety, or well-being of a worker, the employer is liable to pay a fine that is imposed by the court. The Labour Court had jurisdiction over this area of law, and it was one that I was not familiar with before my appointment. When I was faced with such a case, I spent some of my judgment detailing the rules that apply in such matters. Drafting the applicable criteria helped me to establish a list of conditions that I could apply in other cases. I was surprised to learn, many years later, that I was often quoted by judges and justices of the peace sitting in the Criminal and Penal Divisions of the Court of Quebec. I presume this is because I was one of the few judges who rendered their decisions in writing in this area of the law.

While I know that several of my judgments have been followed and quoted, I was most pleased to learn that one of the first judgments that I wrote while I was at the Court of Quebec was followed by a judge in a higher court. You may remember the case previously described: the plaintiff sued after suffering from water infiltration from the roof and elsewhere in the house as well as experiencing electrical and plumbing problems. Typically, in such cases, the purchaser sues the seller. In very few cases does the purchaser sue the inspector instead. The choice is generally one or the other, but in the case I presided over, the purchaser instituted a lawsuit against both the seller and the inspector.

Housing inspectors have been found to be negligent and incompetent in carrying out their pre-purchase inspection when they find, but fail to explore, signs indicating that there are serious problems affecting the property. They are also considered negligent if they note a problematic situation but do not explain to the buyer that understanding the source of the problem requires a more detailed examination.

In my case, the inspector mentioned that there were missing tiles on the roof but did not inform the buyer of the roof's premature aging or the risk of any major problems that could affect the roof. The inspector also failed to mention the visible signs of water damage in the basement and on the garage door. There was no mention of the leaking pipes that resulted in blackened floors in a cupboard and mould on the wall beside the bathtub. Finally, the inspector's report did not indicate any of the various problems with the electrical installations that violated the electrical code and that constituted a danger. In short, the inspector failed to raise any red flags. I held the inspector responsible for the damages resulting from the roof, the plumbing, and the electrical systems that the purchaser encountered after buying her home.

The negligence of the inspector in carrying out his mandate, however, did not let the seller off the hook. Several traces of water infiltration in other parts of the house had been deliberately hidden by fresh paint on the walls. The seller had also carefully hidden any signs of water damage on the floors of the house by installing carpets and other objects to cover the floors. It was obvious that the seller knew about the problems affecting his home and worked hard to hide them from the buyer. By acting as he did, he incurred a share of responsibility. The question was how much?

There was no simple equation I could use to determine the shared responsibility among the faults of the inspector and the seller. In such cases, it is up to the judge to try to arrive at a fair and equitable apportionment, assessing the gravity of each fault. In my case, I split the responsibility of the damages to be paid, ordering the inspector to pay 60 percent and the seller to pay 40 percent.

A CASE GOES PUBLIC

Another case of mine that deserves mention is that of *Centre de la petite enfance La Rose des Vents c Alliance des intervenantes* en *milieu familial Laval, Laurentides, Lanaudière (CSC).*[1] This case involved an appeal from a decision of a labour commissioner who concluded that certain employees of a daycare centre (*des personnes responsables d'un service de garde*) were employees and not independent contractors, and he accordingly certified a union to represent them. The daycare centre, as well as the attorney general of Quebec, appealed the labour commissioner's decision.

My judgment, in appeal, set out the criteria for determining whether or not an individual was considered an employee. After an analysis of their working conditions and the applicable case law, I concluded that the workers in question were definitely employees of the daycare centre and, therefore, that they were entitled to be unionized. Although, for me, the case was simply another appeal file, it was considered a huge victory for the unionization of daycare workers. What surprised me the most was that my judgment was reported in virtually every newspaper in the province of Quebec.

The government was not pleased with my judgment. Rather than attack it in the courts, the government passed a law that had the effect of overturning my decision. I was

---

Chaper 6

1 *Centre de la petite enfance La Rose des Vents c Alliance des intervenantes en milieu familial Laval, Laurentides, Lanaudière (CSQ)*, 2003 CanLII 28444 (QC TT).

disappointed in the government's approach but was at least satisfied that, as judges, we could write a judgment that we considered correct in law and that we were independent of any position that a government could take.

THE BANK FRAUD

While many of my cases followed a similar vein, others were completely outside of my usual purview. The Court of Quebec rarely sees cases involving lawsuits against banks or fraud. Usually, such cases come before the Superior Court where the monetary value of the dispute is far higher than the monetary limits we dealt with at the Court of Quebec. This particular case, which I call the "Bank Fraud," was exceptional because it dealt with both areas—banks and fraud.

A company, which I will call GYM Inc., was a victim of fraud. The company sued its bank for its loss, but the bank maintained that it was not liable. The case was a complex one, and I was intrigued to find out more about the scam that had been perpetrated.

Ms. A., the owner of GYM, sold sports equipment internationally. Her company required that its overseas clients pay for its products by a wire transfer. GYM received an order from a man in the Middle East who had never done business with the company before. The amount in question was very small, less than five thousand dollars. Shortly after placing the order, the client advised Ms. A. by email that he had mistakenly sent a payment of close to seventy thousand US dollars to GYM's account rather than the actual cost of the equipment. After sending his email, he called her every five minutes asking her to immediately return the amount of his overpayment.

The client gave Ms. A. the name and address of the company to whom he wanted the overpayment to be returned. Its corporate name was different from that of the client, but he explained that it was a holding company of his business. Without verifying the identity of the company where she was to send the overpayment, she agreed to return her client's funds as soon as she confirmed that they were in her account.

The following day, GYM's account showed a deposit of the alleged amount of US $69,600 sent by the client. Ms. A. assumed that the funds had arrived by wire transfer, and she authorized her bank to make a rapid wire transfer of sixty-five thousand US dollars to the holding company in question. A little more than a week later, Ms. A. learned that the funds she had seen in her account had not come in by wire transfer after all; they had come in by cheque. She was told that the cheque was not valid, and the bank would charge that amount back to GYM's account. Ms. A. panicked. She traced the cheque and found it had been issued by a bank in a city in the south of the United States. She tried to order a stop payment on her wire transfer, but it was too late.

Ms. A. filed a report with the police, the Royal Canadian Mounted Police, and the police in the Middle Eastern city where her client lived, all without success. She then sued her bank. She claimed that the bank had not taken the most elementary precautions with respect to the cheque; it had failed to hold the funds, it had failed to verify the cheque despite fraud warnings on GYM's account, and it had failed to follow basic procedures.

The evidence showed that there was a note on GYM's account warning tellers to verify any request GYM made to wire out funds. However, the note had nothing to do with verifying cheques, which was how the fraud was accomplished. A client's signature is not required for a bank deposit; the bank had followed all necessary rules in this respect. Ms. A. also claimed that the bank had failed to hold the funds deposited before it transferred funds to its Middle Eastern client. Unfortunately, the bank's policy of holding funds applied only to personal deposit accounts, not to business accounts. Banks have a policy not to interfere with its clients' business transactions, and they even provide provisional credit to a customer's account. A representative of the bank explained that to do otherwise on the grounds that a cheque could possibly be fraudulent would paralyze the pay system.

Finally, Ms. A. claimed the bank made no effort to verify the cheque despite the fact that the deposit memo was not in the most articulate English. It was true that the language on the memo was not perfect. However, it referred to the "deposition of the enclosed instrument," which was comprehensible enough.

During the course of the hearing, I learned a great deal about banking procedures, banking principles and practices, as well as the obligations of banks. In addition, the lawyers representing the two parties were exceptionally skilled; they were knowledgeable, well prepared, and polite not only to me, which is expected, but also to each other.

While I understood Ms. A.'s despair about the loss of funds and the fraud that had taken place, I found that her company was negligent in its handling of the entire affair. GYM showed gross negligence in wiring funds to a company in the Middle East that it did not know, without first taking basic precautions to assure that it had received a wire transfer from its client. It had not verified that the money from the client had in fact been credited to GYM's account by a wire transfer and that the funds were available in its account. The evidence did not show that the bank was responsible for the loss that GYM had incurred. I therefore dismissed the lawsuit.

MEDICAL MALPRACTICE

Cases concerning medical malpractice are also rarely heard in the Court of Quebec. These cases usually involve huge sums of money and are thus handled by the Superior Court. However, on rare occasions, patients sue their doctors and file their lawsuits in the Court of Quebec. One such case was instituted by a woman who claimed that her doctor had removed a vein other than the one she wanted removed.

Ms. B. suffered from varicose veins for many years, and her situation had worsened over time. Her legs were swollen and painful. From an esthetic viewpoint, given that her varicose veins were very visible on her left leg, she was uncomfortable wearing a bathing suit or short dresses. She consulted a doctor specializing in vascular medicine who referred her to a surgeon to operate on her left leg. She underwent the operation, but when the bandages were removed, the vein that had always been visible on her left leg was still present. She complained to her surgeon. He explained that the vein that was removed was inside her left leg and not on the surface. He said that he could not operate on the surface vein.

Ms. B. was very upset. She had undergone the operation for the sole purpose of removing the vein that was visible on the surface of her leg. She sued because of the physical and psychological damages that she suffered as a result of the surgery and claimed compensation.

For the surgeon who had been sued, the outcome was important. Though the amount of the claim was small, his reputation was at stake. The surgeon explained that, according to Ms. B.'s test results, there was a deficiency in the valve of an internal vein that needed to be corrected by a procedure called "stripping." Although this vein is called a superficial vein, it is actually deeper than the veins on the surface of the leg. Those on the surface, which are visible, are called collateral veins.

To succeed in a medical malpractice case, a patient must establish that a physician committed a fault and that the fault was the direct cause of the damages that they suffered. Doctors are held to an obligation called an "obligation of means" and not an "obligation of result," which means that they must act as any reasonably prudent and diligent doctor would if placed in the same circumstances. To establish that the doctor committed a fault, Ms. B. had to show that he committed a diagnostic error and/or used outdated methods or inappropriate tests or that the treatment used was incorrect.

Ms. B.'s surgeon presented an expert witness who explained the nature of the surgery that had been carried out and the fact that the treatment that had been performed was in conformity with the rules of art. He concluded that the surgery was appropriate for her medical condition. In addition, he claimed that, in order to treat the problem of the varicose veins and to resolve the medical deficiency, it was necessary to operate on the large internal vein, known as the superficial vein. The surgeon explained that the visible vein on the surface was the consequence of the problem and not the source of the problem.

Ms. B. had the burden of proof. She had not established that her surgeon had committed any fault with respect to her diagnosis or her treatment. The fact that she was dissatisfied with the surgery was not sufficient to establish that her surgeon had committed any fault with respect to the medical intervention. However, there was one important sticking point: Ms. B. had not been informed that the vein that would be removed was not the one on the surface.

In civil law, doctors are required to provide their patient with information as to the nature of the proposed intervention as well as the possible negative consequences so that the patient can make what we call "an informed decision." When surgery is elective, our courts require that even more complete information be given to the patient. The doctor must not only ensure that the necessary information is transmitted but also that it is understood by the patient. Finally, the doctor must obtain the patient's consent before proceeding to operate, and the consent must be free and informed.

Ms. B. did elect to undergo an operation, but she believed that she was agreeing to an operation that would remove the vein that was visible on her leg. She was embarrassed by its presence and wanted it taken out. Even though she suffered from a deficiency related to the internal vein, and the surgery she did receive was aimed at rectifying the problem of a valve, Ms. B. had no interest in resolving that problem; her sole preoccupation was her appearance. The purpose of her operation, for her, was to have the apparent vein—which caused her so much psychological stress—removed. In short, she wanted to improve her appearance, and this did not happen.

Although the doctor in question treated the medical problem in accordance with the rules of art, I found that he had failed to explain to Ms. B. that the surgery would not remove the visible vein on the surface of her leg. His failure to provide Ms. B. with the necessary information regarding her medical problem and nature of the operation, before carrying out the surgery, constituted a fault. I concluded that he was obliged to compensate his patient for the prejudice that resulted from his failure to respect his obligation to properly inform his patient. In my discretion, I awarded the patient a nominal sum.

THE NEGATIVE LABOUR MARKET OPINION

The Court of Quebec does not deal with all types of issues. Immigration cases, for example, are handled by specialized tribunals—namely, the Immigration and Refugee Board. However, in certain instances involving a monetary claim, specialized fields of law like immigration do come into play in our courtrooms. One such case of mine involved what initially appeared to be a simple claim for a breach of contract but turned out to be far more complex.

The story concerns Mr. R.'s attempt to bring his daughter to Canada to work as a caregiver. He signed a contract with DI, an immigration consulting company, to find an employer for his daughter. The potential employer had to be willing to hire a foreign national. DI found what seemed like a suitable employer, but the prospective employer changed her mind and cancelled her offer. DI then found another prospective employer for R.'s daughter. The paperwork was processed, but, ultimately, the application for a work permit in Canada as a live-in caregiver was refused by the government, allegedly because this second prospective employer had withdrawn his offer of employment.

However, the second prospective employer had not, in fact, withdrawn his offer. DI claimed that Mr. R.'s daughter did not have the necessary qualifications as that was the reason the government gave for the application's rejection. Knowing that she did have the qualifications necessary for the caregiver job, Mr. R. contended that DI had failed to provide the services promised and sought a reimbursement of the cost of hiring the consulting firm.

During the hearing, I learned that officials of both Quebec Immigration and Citizenship and Immigration Canada are involved in the process of hiring a foreign worker. It is not sufficient that the prospective employer's contract of employment and the candidate be approved; a favourable or neutral labour market opinion (LMO) must also be obtained. This means that a study of the labour market is carried out to determine whether a Canadian is available to do the job that is being offered to a foreign national. A favourable LMO is only issued if the foreign worker will not have an impact on the Canadian labour market.

In this case, there had been some confusion with officials because of the two consecutive offers of employment. However, what ultimately led to the refusal of the application of Mr. R.'s daughter was not her lack of qualifications, as the consultant DI contended, but, rather, the LMO. It was determined that it was possible to find a Canadian in the Canadian labour market who could do the job in question. In fact, when the application was denied, the second prospective employer found a local resident who was able to do the work and hired her.

When the LMO is not positive, Immigration Canada considers that the contract of employment is not valid. However, rather than provide this reason for rejecting the application, the government wrote that no employment contract existed. The immigration officer explained that there is nothing in the standard form sent by the government to applicants that corresponds to an absence of a positive LMO and, therefore, that another category is used. In this case, the reason given was the absence of an employment contract. The government's response failed to explain the actual reason that the application was refused and led to the conflict between the parties.

Once I understood how the process worked and what had happened in the file, I still had to decide whether Mr. R.'s claim for reimbursement should be granted or not. After studying the terms of the contract, I concluded that DI had not respected the conditions of the contract. DI had not found an employer in Canada who met the criteria set by the Canadian government to hire a foreign national, which it had been mandated to do. I awarded Mr. R. the reimbursement of the money he had paid DI to find a job for his daughter.

Although this file involved more work and effort than most other cases, it gave me the opportunity to learn about certain aspects of Canada's immigration policy and how it is applied. It was fascinating work, and I appreciated acquiring this new knowledge.

THE LAWYERS

I rarely remembered the names of the lawyers who appeared before me. Perhaps I should, but there were many lawyers who presented cases in the Court of Quebec. With the exception of lawyers who regularly appeared in cases of confinement to a mental institution, most attorneys pleaded before me only once or twice, and I never saw them again.

The lawyers I do remember stood out either for their exceptional performance or for their total lack of competence. Unfortunately, the second case was more common as our court was seen as a good training ground for new lawyers. Since the jurisdiction of the Court of Quebec (at the time when I sat) began at one cent and that of the Superior Court began after seventy thousand dollars,[2] where the jurisdiction of the Court of Quebec ended, it was only natural that the large law firms sent their junior lawyers to the Court of Quebec to learn the ropes. Instead of presenting cases that involved hundreds of thousands of dollars, young lawyers could begin their legal experience with cases where the monetary value was not very high. As a judge, this meant that, at times, it was, necessary to provide guidance to young lawyers who were still in their learning stage of their legal careers.

On occasion, a case was sufficiently important for a law firm that one of their senior lawyers came to plead the case. This occurred in cases such as those involving a lawsuit against a bank, a major real estate transaction, or situations where the reputation of the defendant was on the line. It was always a pleasure to deal with these cases. The lawyers had a command of the facts, the law, and the jurisprudence. They were usually well prepared, articulate, and effective litigators. As well, they raised fewer inappropriate objections and tended to be civil toward each other. I often wished we had more cases involving these experienced attorneys.

THE PARTIES

I also rarely remember the names of the litigants. It has happened on many occasions that someone has come up

---

2 There is now concurrent jurisdiction of the Court of Quebec and the Superior Court for cases where the amount of the claim is between seventy-five thousand dollars and one hundred thousand dollars.

to me at a party, a law society event, or even at a public function and said: “Do you remember me? You heard my case where I sued company ABC.” Since I never recall the names in the cases I heard, I always ask them what their case was about, hoping they had not lost their lawsuit and were not approaching me to complain about the outcome. Invariably, once the nature of the case is mentioned, I know exactly what the case was about.

I had and still have an excellent recall of the facts of most of the cases I heard and their outcomes. There was no reason to remember the names of the lawyers or the names of the parties, which perhaps is why I do not remember them. While I have not retained their names, I do recall many of the litigants who appeared before me. In virtually all of the cases where I remember the people involved, it is because I recall not just the particulars of the case but also the details from the hearing. The cases stand out for various reasons, whether because of the unusual nature of the circumstances involved or because of the way in which the litigants handled themselves during the hearing.

There is one particular case that comes to mind when I think of noteworthy litigants. It was a case where the plaintiff, who was also a lawyer, sued his client for unpaid fees. In such cases, the lawyers generally produce a list of the work that was done, together with their hourly rate, to establish what they claim is owed to them. Typically, the clients who refuse to pay the bill expresses their dissatisfaction with the services rendered.

When judging such cases, I had to determine whether the lawyer was entitled to the fees being claimed. In coming to a decision, I would consider a number of factors, such as whether the client had in fact given a mandate to the lawyer and agreed to the rate charged, whether the nature of the problem was clearly explained to the client, whether the legal work had been carried out, and whether the fees charged were reasonable.

In this case, however, the lawyer in question had represented the mother of a child in a custody case. He presented a motion to the Superior Court of Quebec requesting custody for the mother, whom he was representing, in Quebec. However, a judge in Ontario had previously granted custody on a temporary basis to the child's father. The father, who was living in Ontario, learned about the judgment subsequently rendered in Quebec and succeeded in having the Quebec judgment withdrawn. The lawyer, who appeared more intent on making money than properly representing his client, sent his bill to the mother, who was his client. She refused to pay. She invoked the lawyer's bad faith in instituting proceedings in Quebec without telling her about the Ontario order. She considered that her lawyer knew that the proceedings he had taken on her behalf were useless.

While it is true that a lawyer cannot guarantee the outcome of proceedings that are instituted on behalf of a client, the court takes into consideration any shortcomings on the part of the lawyer. In this case, the lawyer was aware of the proceedings in Ontario and had failed to verify the status of the case in that province. He had not retained a correspondent to keep him informed as to any developments in the file. He also did not attempt to have the order, which had been rendered by the Ontario court, withdrawn before trying to obtain an order from the court in Quebec. He should have done that to ensure that contradictory judgments would not be rendered, which was exactly what occurred in this case.

In addition, the lawyer had not informed his client of the nature of the problem—namely, that the court in Ontario had already rendered a custody order. He did not explain the risks of presenting procedures for custody in Quebec, and he failed to explain that, since identical procedures had been instituted in two provinces, there was a possibility that two contradictory judgments could be rendered. In short, he was disingenuous in handling the case, incompetent, and, in my opinion, an embarrassment to the profession.

At trial, he defended himself poorly, failing to justify his actions. His behaviour reflected his inadequate representation of his client. After hearing the evidence, I concluded that his fees were not warranted. Many hours had been spent uselessly and could have been avoided.

Chapter 7

Communication

When it comes to the law, the stakes are often very high. While the amounts in my judgments may not have been life changing, people's reputations were often on the line. Being able to communicate clearly—in the courtroom and in my judgments—was critical.

Learning French was an essential skill for my career since most of my cases were in that language and I do not think there was a single anglophone among the support staff. The schooling I received to learn the French language was far from adequate. Contrary to many other countries, where students finish their schooling with fluency in a second language, I did not graduate from either high school or McGill University with any fluency in French. Without a solid background in French, it was imperative that I learn the language.

LEARNING IN FRENCH

I grew up as an English speaker at a time when it was not necessary to speak French in Quebec to succeed in a career. However, my father had vision. Well before *le fait Français* (the French fact) became a reality for anglophones in the province of Quebec, my father told me that, if I intended to stay in Quebec, I had to learn French. My brothers left for the West Coast, but I was less adventurous—and more attached to my parents—than they were. I remained in Montreal and went to university in English. After I obtained my undergraduate degree at McGill, my father wanted me to continue my studies at the University of Montreal where all my master-level courses would be in French. I agreed, but I was less than confident about his advice. My elementary school and high school French classes had been far from adequate, and though I considered that I could function in French, I was by no means fluent.

On my first day of class, I lost a contact lens and got down on my hands and knees trying to retrieve it. The professor was rather alarmed by my behaviour and asked me why I was on the floor. I was unable to answer her in French and considered it inappropriate to speak to her in English. I pantomimed the problem, which seemed to work, but I was flustered and embarrassed.

As my classes went on, I struggled to understand anything from my lectures or textbooks. It did help that I was able to study with the chatter of my classmates around me since I could not follow their conversations, but I was very unhappy—not only because of my difficulty understanding my lectures but also because I had no friends. I eventually formed a strong connection with two women in my classes who were also not native born,[1] but it took time.

In those first early months, I wanted to quit. My mother told me that I could abandon the program if that was what I wanted but pointed out that, if I continued my studies, I would at least learn French, even if I did

---

Chapter 7

1 Jocelyne Bonnefils, who came from Haiti, and Norma Heloua, who was Palestinian, became my close friends during our program.

not learn speech therapy and audiology. It was the best advice I could have received. When I began my studies at the University of Montreal, I struggled to carry on a basic conversation in French. In the end, I finished with a fluency in French, without which my career would have never been what it was.

FRENCH TELEVISION

After obtaining a position at the Canada Labour Relations Board, I had to move to Ottawa. I purchased a house there and modified it, creating additional living space on the ground floor to improve the eventual resale value of the house. When one of my colleagues asked if I was interested in renting out a room to a friend of hers, I was reluctant at first. She swore it would be a temporary arrangement until her friend could find permanent lodging, so I eventually agreed. Chantal Sauriol, a lawyer from Montreal working for the federal Justice Department in Ottawa, came to see the house. After a number of discussions about her concerns regarding the safety of the area (it was very safe, but she was unfamiliar with the area and was not sure) and the duration of the lease (neither of us wanted a long-term lease), we came to an agreement, and Chantal moved into my house.

What started off as a good arrangement worked out better than either of us had anticipated. Chantal and I kept different hours except for a short time in the evening when we fell into the habit of watching television together. She insisted on watching in her language, which was French. I accepted, albeit reluctantly, because she was cooking dinner for both of us. Over a few years, I regularly watched several well-known programs that she had chosen.

Little did I know, given that I was working in English at the time, how beneficial it would be for me to maintain my understanding of French.

THE CHALLENGE OF FRENCH IN COURT

French is the official language in the province of Quebec, and when I began sitting in the Court of Quebec, virtually all of my cases were held in French. Although I was very comfortable in the language, it was only when I started hearing cases that I realized I did not have as full a command of French vocabulary as I thought I had. I had never had a discussion with anyone in French about a number of subjects that arose in my hearings. For example, a description of a lake filled with water lilies left me perplexed, and I had certainly never discussed the parts of a car's engine in French.

The language issue was most problematic in construction cases. I did not even know the vocabulary in English, so I certainly did not know the terms in French. The problem was compounded by the fact that I did not know which words I should know, and would certainly know their English counterparts, as opposed to technical terms that I would not be expected to know in either language. For example, it was completely understandable for me not to know the meaning of the word "*contreventement*," which is a wooden structure into which cement is poured prior to the cement solidifying, but it would be unacceptable not to know the meaning of the word "*bardeaux*," which are shingles on a roof, or "*marteau*," which is a hammer.

Since I did not want to appear as if my fluency was inadequate, I could not ask the parties what any particular term meant. Instead, I wrote down and underlined the words I didn't understand and put a question mark in the margins of my notebook. Sometimes, although I tried to mask my reactions, the parties noted that I looked puzzled and would either ask whether I understood their testimony or offer an explanation without asking me if I needed it. On occasion, Josette, my court clerk, who sat in front of me, would write the term in English on a slip of paper, turn around, and pass me the translation. She was a godsend. She knew when I did not understand without my saying a word.

Given that I began working as a judge before the advent of Google, the process of looking up numerous words in an English French dictionary at the end of each hearing was very tedious. Fortunately, the number of words I needed to translate gradually decreased over time. By the time I retired, I had an extensive vocabulary not only in construction matters but also in virtually all areas of endeavour.

At the time that I sat as a judge, lawsuits could be drafted and pleaded in English or French. All judges were required to be bilingual and be able to preside over cases in either language. Therefore, translators were assigned only if one or both parties spoke neither English nor French. Lawyers who litigate in Montreal are, for the most part, bilingual. There may be fewer bilingual lawyers outside this large urban area where English is less commonly used, but this was not a factor in my cases. With the introduction of new legislation by the Quebec government in 2022, the situation changed dramatically. All proceedings and contracts must be drafted in French. At the time of writing, this legislation is being challenged, and it remains to be seen what the outcome will be.

When I was on the bench, given that the parties and their witnesses could testify in whichever of the two languages they chose, it was not unusual to have one party present their case in French and the other party in English. If either party did not understand the opposing party or their witnesses, that person was obliged to get a translator; it was not the role of the judge to translate for a party or a witness nor the role of the other party. I sometimes found it strange to hear one of the two parties claim they did not understand the language of the other party, although they had concluded a contract together and had dealings with each other in, presumably, a shared language. Nevertheless, in all probability, it was the limited language skills of one of the parties that led to a misunderstanding between them and, ultimately, to the lawsuit.

Judgments are issued only in one language, unless one of the parties asks the court for a translation. Therefore, in cases that are presented in both languages, it is up to the judge to choose which language to use for the judgment. I usually asked the parties at the beginning of such a case if they had a preference. If both parties agreed upon a language, I wrote the decision in that language. If the parties disagreed, I would write the judgment in the language of the party that lost the case. It seemed only fair for the losing party to understand why they had lost their lawsuit. The winning party would be satisfied simply to know that they won.

The only problem I had with such an approach was the dilemma of what language to use when I began drafting. Since I began writing immediately at the end of each hearing day, and hearings often stretched over several days, it was extremely rare to know at the end of the first or even the second day how I would decide and which party would lose. There were some instances where I began to write in one language and, when I reached a decision, had to go back and rewrite my draft in the other language.

Although my comprehension continues to be excellent, and I am very comfortable speaking French, writing in that language has always been more of a challenge for me. I believe that written French is difficult to master. That being said, my language skills necessarily became better and better as time went on. I quickly learned many standard phrases that are regularly found in judgments. When Josette, my assistant, corrected my drafts, I noted the changes she made and tried to remember them. Reading the judgments of others also helped.

Ultimately, I wrote with ease, but I nevertheless always wanted my texts to be looked over by a keen set of eyes. I would have been embarrassed if there were ever any grammatical or spelling errors in my judgments. Fortunately, I did not have to worry. Josette, who corrected my texts, had such a mastery over her native French language that I frequently received compliments about my French judgments.

THE CARPET CASE

It was very unusual for anyone to raise the subject of any judge's understanding of English or French. However, it did occur in one of my cases. The plaintiff had purchased a carpet on a trip to Tunisia. When he returned home, he believed that he had been the victim of a fraudulent transaction. He sued his travel agent, claiming that the agent was responsible for the fraud he had suffered—namely, that the carpet was not the one he had chosen but, rather, one that was used and had little value.

According to the evidence, the conditions governing the trip clearly stated that the agent had no responsibility for the quality of excursions and for any of its clients' personal purchases or expenses. Although the travel agent had organized the excursion to the town where the plaintiff had purchased his carpet, the agent could not guarantee the quality of any items that were bought from local merchants. I quickly dismissed the action. I stated that the travel agent could not be held responsible for the conformity of the items bought by his clients when the clients decided on their own to buy the products.

The plaintiff filed a complaint claiming that I did not understand the French language. I wrote a short reply to the Council of the Quebec Judiciary stating that I was fluent in French, having studied and worked in that language. Although I have an accent, I pointed out that my comprehension was excellent, and if a particular word or expression arose during a hearing that I was not familiar with, I would have no hesitation to ask for its meaning. I maintained that I had fully understood the evidence in the case and had felt no need to ask any qualifying questions. I considered that the plaintiff's submission was, in reality, an appeal of my judgment. The Council of Judges, which examined the complaint, was of the same opinion and dismissed it.

A RUMOUR

It is important to communicate a decision in such a way that the parties understand not only the outcome of a case but also how the decision was reached. One of my colleagues wrote a judgment and instructed their assistant to issue the judgment to the parties. Then, the judge had a change of mind and asked the assistant to type the alternate version, retrieve the first version from the registry office, and issue the alternate version in its place. What the judge sought to do was not in itself problematic. However, when the steps were not followed in the proper order, it was disastrous.

The assistant did type a second version, as required, and sent it to the registry to be issued. But she did so before getting the first version back. The assistant asked the registry office to return the first judgment in order to destroy it, but some delay—not to mention confusion—must have taken place in the administration of the file in the registry office. The second version of the judgment was transmitted to the parties but only after the first version had already been sent to them. Needless to say, what occurred was embarrassing both for the judge and the court. The gaffe was covered up as much as possible, but it could not be entirely concealed. I heard about the events through the staff, who are often privy to matters that are not reported to the other judges.

There never was an official version of this story. Perhaps it was just a rumour.

Chapter 8

Finding Support

While it was important to speak French in my career, it was just as important to have adequate support, both professionally and personally. The support in my position as a judge came from various sources and included our legal services, our information technology (IT) department, colleagues, and experts who appeared in some cases. Most important was the support of my husband and my assistant. This chapter details each of their contributions that facilitated my life on the bench.

BJØRN

Bjørn and I met when I was working at the Canada Labour Relations Board. A friend contacted me and asked if I wanted to meet someone who was looking for a ski partner. I said that I was interested, provided that he could keep up with me! I was a very good downhill skier and was not interested in waiting for someone struggling to get down an expert slope. My friend told me that the name of the person in question was Bjørn. I wrote down his name as "Bur-in" (which I called him for many years and, to his ears, still do today). I phoned him, and we arranged to ski together when I returned to Montreal on the weekend. We went skiing at Jay Peak in Vermont, just across the border in the United States. To my delight, Bjørn was not only an excellent skier but was also very bright, interesting, and excellent company, which was important since the trip to and from the ski hill involved a two-hour drive each way.

Bjørn and I skied together for two winters. He was my platonic ski buddy, and the arrangement suited both of us, or so I thought. At the end of the second season of skiing, however, Bjørn asked me if I wanted to go to a movie with him sometime. He then specified that he was referring to that weekend. I accepted. I was rather curious as to what he looked like in regular clothing since I had only seen him in a ski suit. We began seeing each other regularly after that, although I had no idea that what began as a casual relationship would develop into something more.

Both before and after our marriage, Bjørn was an essential part of my unofficial team. When I returned from a day in court, I almost always related my cases to him at suppertime. He was a good listener and was my sounding board. Talking about the facts of a case aloud, without naming the parties, often helped me to reach a decision.

On one occasion, when his sister was visiting us from Norway, I was describing one of my cases to her. Bjørn intervened to add a fact to my story. My sister-in-law was taken aback and asked how it was that Bjørn was aware of the facts of the case. She wondered whether he attended my hearings. I explained that he was never present but heard about most of my cases. While I have told others that Bjørn often pretends to listen to me but, in reality, tunes me out, I know that he actually listened to the details of my trials.

Josette corrected my French but not my English. Bjørn, although born and raised in Norway, has an excellent command of the English language, and he proofread my judgments when they were written in English. It was important to me that they be readily understandable. If I had written any text that was not clear to him, it certainly would not be clear to the parties and their lawyers, who were the ultimate readers. He was an important critic in this regard. Even more important was his knowledge of virtually all technical matters. His engineering and business background, together with his knowledge about cars, construction matters, computers, taxation, and many other areas of endeavour was of a tremendous help to me. This was particularly true in the Small Claims Court cases where parties were not represented by lawyers and often did not hire expert witnesses to explain the problem concerned in their file.

Although every decision in my cases was mine alone to make, I often asked Bjørn to explain the technical aspects that were not clear to me. After I followed his drawings or his explanations, I always had a better grasp of the issue in dispute. Often, he would provide me with a concrete example of what was only orally described at the hearing. For example, he showed me the solid type of plumbing we had under the sinks in our house when various types of different tubing were described in a case in which flooding had occurred. In other instances, he would bring me to his workshop or to the garage to show me what a particular type of machine looked like or how some piece of equipment worked. He would even make drawings with the component parts involved in a car, a building, or other products and provide explanations for how they worked.

One of my cases involved a computer repair for which the defendant refused to pay. I had never caught up with computer technology, and I was at a loss about whether or not the repair performed had been the correct course of action. Before I heard the case, I asked Bjorn to explain the role of the various parts of the machine. Bjørn drew a diagram and explained what possible causes there are when a computer does not work as it should as well as what must be done in each instance for it to function properly. His explanations allowed me to understand the work done by the computer repairperson. I must admit that, in the absence of his explanations, I am not sure that I would have been able to follow the explanations given in court and render a decision that was correct.

Without expert witnesses to explain certain technical matters in the Small Claims Court, it was not always easy to fully comprehend the problems we were presented with. I often wonder how many cases are wrongly decided when a judge fails to grasp the complex technical realities of a case in the absence of an expert.

I was fortunate not only for Bjørn's language and technical skills but also for all his other attributes, particularly his patience. I would often work late at the office, coming home at 7:30 or 8:00 in the evening. He never complained about my working hours. Rather, he made life easier for me by purchasing our food and cooking dinner so that our meals were ready when I arrived home. He took care of so many aspects of our lives, allowing me the luxury of spending whatever time I needed to read, think, and write judgments. He enjoyed and still enjoys cooking, planning, organizing, and fixing anything that is not functional. Bjørn is my best friend and my partner for life; I married a gem.

JOSETTE

When I was at the Quebec Labour Court and the secretary I had been assigned left for another position, I needed a new assistant. I was eager to find someone who wrote French exceptionally well in order to assure that my judgments did not contain the spelling mistakes that I often made in French.

I interviewed several candidates from among the potential candidates before Josette, a well-dressed, elegant, and attractive woman, arrived in my office. She appeared to be assured and had a very pleasing personality. Josette was bright, college educated, and had worked for a publishing company. Most importantly, she wrote impeccable French. I hoped that she would do well on the tests I had given to each applicant, and she did. I hired her enthusiastically and never looked back.

Josette came with me when I was transferred to the Civil Division of the Court of Quebec and remained my assistant until the end of my career on the bench. Her transfer to the Court of Quebec with me was both a plus and a minus. A plus because she ensured that my judgments were issued in exceptionally good French and also because we had already developed an excellent relationship by that point and continued to work well together over the years. The minus was because I was new and was not familiar with many aspects of the work involved at the court. A knowledgeable assistant could have helped bridge that gap, but Josette also had no experience in this court. In the early months, she was unable to help with some of the administrative aspects of the job. However, we both eventually learned the workings of the court.

Over the years, Josette was an invaluable help. I made numerous errors in my written judgments, even with a grammar and spelling check application installed on my computer. Josette corrected my texts so professionally that the final version of my judgments read as if it had been written not only by a francophone but also by a francophone who wrote very well.

Josette considered us a team, and we were. As was generally the case, she was my court clerk as well as my assistant and was present with me at all my hearings. Since she was (and is) a very intelligent woman, she had opinions about most cases and voiced them without reservation. I sometimes thought she would have liked to render the decisions herself! It was not uncommon for her to type comments on my draft judgments, either in brackets or in bold characters. Many were pertinent. At other times, I was struck by her audacity in telling me that I was clearly wrong. In one of my insurance cases, she not only indicated that she did not agree with my decision, but she also pointed to the evidence and her analysis of it to substantiate her point of view. Obviously, the decision was mine. Although I appreciated her thoughts on the matter, I did not change my mind. Her input in my cases was nevertheless useful, and, in one case, it was a godsend.

While correcting my French in a draft decision, Josette asked me where my conclusions were on the cross demand[1] in the case. I realized that, while I had dealt with the cross demand in the body of the judgment, inadvertently, I had not included my decision about this aspect of the case in my conclusions. Her reminder saved me the embarrassment of having to issue a rectified judgment that would have included the conclusions about both the lawsuit and the cross demand.

We had a relationship that was not common at the courthouse. Contrary to the prevailing situation with the

Chapter 8

1 A cross demand is a claim presented by a defendant (who is sued) against the plaintiff (who is the party who instituted the lawsuit).

other judges and their assistants, our relationship was not that of a superior and an employee. We spoke daily when I was drafting judgments at home, not only about my cases but also about books, movies, and travel. It was not unusual for her to call me to tell me about a television program or a book she thought would interest me. We often ate lunch together at court and discussed my cases, current events, fashion, and various other issues, including personal matters.

Josette had a great sense of humour, and we regularly laughed together. At one point, I told her she could address me by my first name rather than "Madame" Handman. She declined, explaining that she considered it important to have some distance in our relationship. Given that one of our discussions had involved push-up bras, among other personal matters, I was surprised by her reaction. But Josette continued to address me by my family name, and I respected her choice.

Having a good relationship with an assistant is so important in the life of a judge. Judges and their assistants spend more time in the same premises than spouses, and not every pairing runs smoothly. In fact, I remember several instances where assistants left one judge to work for another, hoping to find a better fit. Sometimes it was the judge's decision, and sometimes it was the decision of the assistant.

After I retired, I was asked about Josette by another judge who was seeking a new assistant. I told him that Josette was heads and shoulders above all the other assistants. He hired her, and I understand they worked together well, though they likely never had any conversations about push-up bras. I consider myself fortunate to have found someone to work with who not only was invaluable at work but who also became a friend and has remained so even after my retirement.

LEGAL AND IT SERVICES

Other sources of support came from our legal and IT services. As in other courts, we had a dedicated legal department. I had experience dealing with such services at the Canada Labour Relations Board and at the Quebec Labour Court, but the services at the Court of Quebec were not entirely analogous.

At the Canada Labour Relations Board, we were not only able to obtain extensive research on any question that we raised, but we could also request a written legal opinion. The resulting texts were often so complete and detailed that some of my colleagues actually took the core of the document and integrated it into their decision. The Quebec Labour Court was at the other extreme. We never received a written opinion from the legal department, and we would not even be given an analysis of the jurisprudence. We were simply provided with the cases to read ourselves.

The service at the Court of Quebec was somewhere between these two extremes, although, thankfully, it was closer to the board's services. We could ask for and receive a list of cases or an analysis of the law regarding a particular situation. If needed, we could also ask for a legal opinion. However, since there were not many lawyers available in the legal department to deal with our requests, this process could be slow. We most often asked for a summary of the state of the law rather than a written legal opinion. The latter took time, and we all wanted the research done "by yesterday." I often heard complaints from colleagues about the length of time it took for the legal department to process their requests, but the criticism seemed unfair to me. Some judges would make a request at the end of the day and then expect to receive a response the following morning! Each judge considered his request to be of paramount importance.

My experience was different. I had become friendly with Maître Renée Desrosiers de la Nauze, the head of the legal department. My friendship was genuine; it was not to obtain any advantages. It was only later, when I heard complaints from my colleagues about how slow the service was, that I realized that I may have been getting preferential treatment. Invariably, when I called legal services, I was asked how quickly I needed a response. When I did need to obtain an opinion quickly, I never failed to get it. However, I believe that I experienced a treatment that differed from my colleagues because of my appreciation of the work being done and the lawyers doing it. I never asked for work to be done quickly unless I had a real urgency, and I always expressed my gratitude to the particular lawyer who had handled my request. Apparently, this was not always the case with other judges.

When I dealt with legal services, it was generally because I was seeking the state of the law on a specific subject. At times, I would ask if there were any decisions on the subject in issue. On some occasions, I would tell the lawyer doing the research how I wanted to decide a case and ask if there were any cases that would support my position. Sometimes, I would simply sit with Maître de la Nauze at lunch and brainstorm with her. I always appreciated our legal service department, particularly when I first began sitting and had so much to learn.

I also made good use of the court's IT department. For many issues involving the use of my computer, my assistant

Josette was able to help me. However, there were times, particularly when I was working at home, when I ran into some technical trouble and needed help. I could contact our IT department and the person I was dealing with could access my computer remotely and talk me through the difficulty. Although my computer skills were far more advanced than when I first saw a computer in my office and refused to turn it on, I was nevertheless happy to have the IT department as support. Computer skills did not come easily to me.

Our computers were secure and were accessible only by those within the court system. We were not only able to email and communicate with our assistants and other judges, but we were also able to access various research sites. In addition, we could log into court recordings and listen to a part or an entire court case. This was useful in instances when our notes were inadequate, when we wished to be certain of the actual words expressed by a witness, and when we wanted to listen again to the legal arguments made at trial.

COLLEAGUES

It was not easy for me to fit into the Court of Quebec. When I first started working there, I found the massive files assigned to me and the procedures daunting since I had virtually no experience practising civil law. This meant that I often spent my lunch hours reading my *Civil Code*[2] and case law and trying to understand my files. I could not relax enough to enjoy a meal with others or participate in their lunchtime conversations, which was where the majority of socializing took place between judges.

2 *Civil Code of Québec*, CQLR c CCQ-1991.

However, I had one friend at the court when I arrived; Eliana Marengo had studied law with me at the University of Montreal. I found her to be sympathetic and someone I could relate to. There were times when, in the privacy of her office, I could let my hair down and allow my tears of frustration to show. Another colleague who became a friend was Juanita Westmoreland Traoré. We met at the first annual judges' conference that I attended. Juanita is Black, and when I first introduced myself, she said: "The Court now has one token Black and one token Jew." We immediately bonded and remained friends.

I have already mentioned my friendship with Renée Desrosiers de la Nauze. At the beginning of my transfer, I often needed help with my files. I should have been consulting with my colleagues, but because of my pride and the absence of a mentor, I chose to consult with Renée. I found her to be not only most helpful but also a genuinely nice person. I invited her to lunch to thank her for all of her help. She told me that, in all the years she had been at the court, it was only the second time she had gone to lunch with a judge. There was clearly a hierarchy at the court, one that I had no interest in maintaining. Over the course of my career at the court, I ate regularly with Renée, and we ultimately became good friends.

It took me much longer to become friendly with my colleagues than most new judges who arrived at the court with similar legal backgrounds and legal experience as that of the sitting judges. This facilitated the development of friendships between them, while, in my case, there was little commonality. Although I had few friends early on, as my knowledge of civil law grew and my ease in sitting in the Court of Quebec gradually increased, I was able to begin establishing relationships.[3] By the time I retired, there were a number of colleagues whose company I enjoyed and with whom I became friendly. Many have remained friends since my retirement.

MENTORS

Every new judge is assigned a senior judge to act as their mentor. The mentor is supposed to assist and oversee the work of the new judge for as long as supervision is needed. Often a close bond forms between a new judge and his mentor. Unfortunately, the mentorship relationship did not work out for me. Since I had virtually no experience in handling civil law cases, I needed a mentor more than most other new judges. Despite this, although I was assigned a mentor, we met on only two occasions, and the judge was of little help either time. I was so overwhelmed with my lack of knowledge in the area of civil law that I did not even know what questions to ask.

The first time I approached my mentor, it was to ask how to handle the issue of costs at the end of my judgment. In civil cases, the winning party obtains all or part of the monetary amount they are seeking as well as the court fees that are payable for the filing, production, or issue of pleadings or documents. I had no idea how to determine how and when costs applied since, in labour law cases, we never ordered the losing party to pay any amount of money consisting of legal costs. My mentor did not understand what I needed in terms of information and simply told me that I was to order the losing party to pay

3 My friendships included David Cameron, Marie Michèle Lavigne, Martine Tremblay, and (the late) Michèle Pauzé.

the legal costs involved. The answer was of little help to me, and I had to consult a member of the legal service.

I was also hampered by embarrassment. I felt, without justification, that my questions were too elementary, and I was reluctant to approach my mentor with them. I even hesitated to ask my other colleagues, for that matter. In one instance, I ventured out of my comfort zone and asked a colleague what was meant by a "contract of adhesion."[4] Instead of explaining the concept, which I had probably learned during my studies but had long forgotten, the judge turned to me and, in a most condescending manner, exclaimed: "You should go back to law school!"

I felt as if I had been abandoned. The person who had been assigned to assist me never checked in to see what I needed and was not there to help me adjust to my new situation. I was left to struggle on my own. When I needed help, I sought it from the legal department, first from one of the junior lawyers and then from the head of the department.

Later, when I had far more knowledge of civil law and wanted to discuss my position in a case with a colleague, I chose my own mentor—namely, François Bousquet—who occupied the office immediately down the hall. He was both competent and friendly. I learned a great deal from him and always appreciated his insight and his help.

EXPERTS

A judge's expertise is limited to the law. Even in situations where a judge is very knowledgeable about a situation

4 A contract of adhesion is a standard-form contract between two parties where the terms and conditions are set by one of the parties and the other party, who is in a weaker position, has little or no ability to change them.

because of his experience, we are not permitted to consider any personal knowledge. This is where experts come into play.

Expert witnesses are persons who have specialized knowledge or experience in a particular field and who will be able to guide the court in areas where it does not have the required knowledge. Most typically, experts are called upon to testify on technical or scientific matters. Regular witnesses are only able to testify as to the facts they are personally aware of and cannot give an opinion. An expert witness, on the other hand, can evaluate a file or listen to the witnesses during the trial and provide an opinion on the matter at issue.

The role of an expert is to explain an issue to enable the judge to understand and better appreciate a particular area in dispute. However, in order to provide that opinion, the court must first recognize the witness as an expert in the expert's field. To determine the status of such a witness, the lawyer who is presenting the expert questions the witness about his education, training, and experience. The opposing lawyer may ask the witness questions as well, but he would only do this in an attempt to discredit the expert. After the questioning, the judge determines whether he considers the witness to be an expert who is permitted to provide his opinion. Irrespective of the testimony presented, the court is not bound by the opinion of the expert. The evaluation of the evidence and the judgment to be rendered in every case is for the judge alone to decide.

One would think that, faced with a given technical or scientific issue, every expert would come to the same conclusion with respect to the cause of the problem before the court and the means of rectifying it. Experts should serve a most useful purpose. However, in virtually every case I heard where experts were involved, the experts of the two opposing parties had differing opinions and came to different conclusions concerning the issue in dispute. It seems to me that the "experts," while supposedly neutral and qualified to assist the court, generally fail to fulfill their role.

This situation comes about because each party hires their own expert. Each expert invariably adopts the position that is favourable to the party who has hired and paid him. The judge then has two conflicting opinions and must pick one of them, without having the necessary technical knowledge to make an informed decision.[5] It is rather disconcerting for a judge to listen to two people who have diametrically opposed views testifying, for example, as to the security of a building's structure, the cause and extent of the damages suffered, the conformity of a construction job to recognized standards, and so on. In light of this situation, one should ask what, then, is the purpose of experts?

Perhaps the best system is that used systematically in the courts of Norway. In that country, the court hires the expert. That person then does not act on behalf of either party but actually explains the technicalities of the situation to the court and assists the court in its understanding of a complex issue. There, the expert witness is much more likely to fulfill the role that we expect of an expert witness in our courts here.

---

5 Since the time I sat on the bench, the *Code of Civil Procedure*, CQLR c C-25, has changed. The new *Code of Civil Procedure* states at s 240 that if conflicting expert reports are filed, the parties may call the experts to a meeting so that they can reconcile their opinions, identify the points on which they differ, and, if necessary, prepare an additional report. The court, even on its own initiative, can order the experts to meet and file an additional report within a specified time.

Chapter 9

My Life as a Judge outside of Court

Judges, like everyone else, have a personal life outside of court. Judges have families and relationships, they travel, and they participate and plan various events and activities during their careers. My experience in this regard was no different. During my time on the bench, I purchased and renovated a home, married my significant other, travelled extensively, hosted dinner parties, and kept in touch with my family and many friends, all while working extremely hard.

Although experiences from everyday life can impact our judgments, if we are not careful to avoid their influence, our experience in court can also affect our everyday life. In this chapter, I talk about both scenarios. There were cases in which I had to set aside my personal reaction based on what I had experienced outside court, and there were instances in my daily activities when the cases I had heard in court provided me with useful knowledge.

THE WEDDING SHOES

My professional life while I was a judge on the Quebec Labour Court was a most pleasant period and relatively uneventful. My personal life, on the other hand, changed considerably during this period. After I moved back to Montreal from Ottawa to assume my functions on the court, I purchased a house, renovated it, and moved in. Shortly afterwards, my then significant other, Bjørn Ellingsen, moved in with me. This required an adaptation that I did not anticipate, but we eventually worked out the kinks of co-habiting and even got married.

I had been sitting at the Court of Quebec for less than two years when Bjørn and I decided to marry and planned our wedding. I was working 24/7, and, in retrospect, I am not sure how I found the time to find a site for the event, buy a wedding dress, compile a guest list, decide on the menu, and deal with all the other items involved in planning a wedding. My then future husband, who is very much a hands-on guy, refused to hire a wedding planner and did a large part of that work himself.

Had it not been for my trouble finding shoes for the wedding that were comfortable, no one at court would have known that I planned to get married. My search for shoes gave away my happy, but undisclosed, event. After going to several stores in the city and being unable to find any shoes that were comfortable, I decided to order them online. I could buy as many pairs as I wanted and return any that did not fit. Happy that I had found a solution, I ordered and returned many pairs of shoes. Given that no one was home to receive the orders, which all arrived during the day, I sent all of the shoes directly to the courthouse.

What I had not anticipated was that, since the public has no access to the judges' area of the court, someone had to open the door when each of the packages arrived. Several times, one of my colleagues just happened to arrive at the door of our area at the same time as the delivery. She ended up bringing me package after package of shoes. Few at the courthouse were aware of my wedding plans as I had planned a small wedding and had not invited any of the judges. However, I had to explain to this colleague why so many packages were arriving at the courthouse.

Because of the shoe deliveries, my wedding plans were no longer a secret, and I was pleased to receive congratulations from many of my peers.

CAR RENTALS

My husband and I travelled regularly, and that often involved a car rental. Because I would spend so much time reading a contract before we rented a car on our trips, and because of my attempts to make changes to the contracts, my husband insisted on dealing with car rentals on his own without my input. However, with the exception of car rentals, I read (and still read) every document I am given, before signing them, even if I am assured that it is a boilerplate contract. I counsel others to do the same. Perhaps because of the many cases I presided over where the defendants failed to read the terms and conditions of the contract they signed, I have always been particularly vigilant when I personally sign any agreement.

There have been drawbacks to this caution. There were situations where I did not agree with various clauses in a contract covering a transaction. However, there are printed contracts that companies impose on their clients, and the terms cannot be changed. When I tried to change a few of the conditions in the case of a bicycle trip I had planned to take, for instance, the company told me that either I sign their contract or I was not welcome to come on the tour. Despite my reservations, I signed the contract as it stood.

Although I was very diligent in carefully reading the contents of a document I signed, many people constantly sign documents they are asked to sign without reading the text. Unfortunately, there are consequences for acting imprudently.

READ WHAT YOU SIGN

One case that stands out in my mind is that of a mother who had signed, as a surety or guarantee, for a loan her daughter had contracted at a bank. When the loan became due, the daughter failed to repay the money she had borrowed, and the bank sued the mother. By signing the loan agreement as a surety, the mother had legally undertaken to pay for the loan in the event that her daughter defaulted.

The mother claimed that she did not understand what she had agreed to when signing the document. According to her explanation, she had signed the contract only to allow her daughter to obtain the loan. In essence, the mother's defence was that she had not given her consent since there was "an error on the nature of the undertaking that she had signed"—that is, she was mistaken about what she had signed. However, the mother had testified that she was anxious to return to work and had not read the contract and or even asked for any explications about its nature. I concluded that her failure to read the contract and obtain any information about her obligations was not an acceptable defence; it amounted to what we consider to be "an inexcusable error" on the part of the signer.

In another case, a man, who had received a lump sum from a pharmaceutical group as start-up capital when he purchased one of their pharmacies, was sued for the reimbursement of this sum after he had sold the business since he had not respected his contractual obligations.

The pharmacist contended that he had only read the contract quickly before signing it; he had little time to do so since he had to return to the office. However, his failure to study the contract was not an excuse. He had received a copy of the contract beforehand and had ample time to study it, pose questions, verify the terms, and try to negotiate the conditions, if possible. The pharmacist had signed a business contract that was legible and clear. The defendant, as the purchaser, had the obligation to take cognizance of all the applicable conditions. The amount he received at the outset to organize the premises and run the pharmacy was not a donation. I concluded that he was required to reimburse the sum he had received.

A JUDGE'S INFLUENCE

I am aware that many of my colleagues used their title as a means of obtaining access to people or to services that they would not otherwise have had. I often noted that a number of assistants in the courthouse would call to make a lunch reservation for "Judge so and so," knowing that they were more likely to get a coveted table that way. I often had occasion to hear a head waiter welcome a judge entering a restaurant by addressing him as *Votre seigneurie* or addressing her as *Madame le juge* (Your Honour or Madam Justice). If the title of judge was being used for restaurant reservations, I can only presume those colleagues of mine were comfortable using it on other occasions as well. For my part, it was a practice I tried to avoid. I did not indicate that I was a judge when I called for an appointment, a reservation, or when I wanted to speak to someone unless it was a professional matter such as that concerning a court file. I do, however, remember one notable exception to that rule.

Josette had received a parking ticket while she was on vacation in New York. She had paid the fine when she was notified; however, despite her diligence in respecting her obligation to pay the fine, she continued to receive notices regarding her ticket. Not only was she advised of the amount payable for the ticket, but she was also charged interest on the fine. She attempted to resolve the matter by calling the department in question, but she was told that no payment had been received. In desperation, she asked for my help.

I called the concerned department and got the same answer. However, I knew for a fact that Josette had paid the fine; I had seen her proof of payment as well as her proof of having mailed her payment. I was determined to find out what happened to her funds, which had been sent to New York via Canada Post. I called the post office, but I was unable to obtain any information from those persons to whom I spoke. I then called the head office in Ottawa.

After getting the run around, I finally asked to speak to the person responsible for their entire operation—this time using my title. I was immediately put in contact with one of the most senior people at Canada Post, who listened to me politely as I explained the problem. After providing the necessary information, the senior manager was able to follow the paper trail and provide me with the evidence of payment. I sent that to the parking enforcement company in New York and was able to resolve the problem.

I was pleased to have been able to put an end to an issue that was causing an ongoing problem for Josette. At the same time, I felt that it was not fair that I was able to obtain a particular service only because I had said that I was "Judge so and so." It was clear that the same treatment would not have been available to everyone, notably Josette herself. I recognized that I was in a privileged position but, at the same time, considered that life is not always fair. On the other hand, if I could use my privilege to help someone in need, I would do so.

WORK WAS ON MY MIND

Most of the time, unless I was on holiday, my work was on my mind. This was particularly so if I had not resolved how I would decide a given case. I was not alone in this respect. Very often, when judges got together at lunch or at the end of the day, they would consult each other about a case or a legal issue that was causing them difficulty. Sometimes, they simply needed a sounding board. On other occasions, they sought confirmation for the position they intended to adopt or the advice of a trusted colleague. It was not only new judges who sought the views of others but also judges who had been on the bench for many years.

In addition to the informal get-togethers in each other's offices, we had regularly scheduled lunch meetings where problematic issues could be raised and discussed by everyone present. These meetings were voluntary, but it was a good occasion to deal with new questions that arose in hearings or unresolved problems in cases and get the advice of colleagues.

There was little urgency to render a judgment immediately. After hearing a case, as I have mentioned, we had up to six months to issue the reasons for judgment in civil cases and four months to render a decision in cases heard in the Small Claims Court. Thus, if I had not decided what the outcome would be in any particular case, there was a considerable amount of time to reach a decision. Still, the longer I sat with a case, the more it distracted me. Even though there was no rush to reach a decision, I would not be able to stop thinking about the case until I had decided what the outcome would be. If I woke during the night, the unresolved case was the first thought I had, and, at times, I would lie awake thinking about it, unable to fall back to sleep. On occasion, I wrote the reasons for the judgment in my mind at night and set it to paper the next day.

There were certain exceptions to the length of time I had to deliberate, as, for example, when I was dealing with objections. However, as I have already explained, even in such instances where one party wanted to block the testimony of the other party and did so by raising an objection, the objection did not have to be decided immediately. If I had not determined how I would deal with the objection, I could take it under advisement and rule on it in the context of my judgment.

On the other hand, there were occasions when I told the parties, in a trial of several days, that I would provide an answer to an objection that was raised by the following day. This gave me time at the end of the hearing that day to research the issue or think about what my ruling would be. Sometimes, I went to bed not having resolved the question. That would often lead to a sleepless night. Even though I fell asleep without difficulty, if I woke up during the night, I would find myself distracted by my dilemma and sleep badly for the rest of the night.

Thankfully, several of my colleagues were early birds. I knew I could knock on their doors before getting ready for another day in court and brainstorm with them. Invariably, as the expression goes, two heads are better than one, and whatever difficulty I had would be worked out before heading back into the courtroom.

THE BAGGAGE JUDGES BRING WITH THEM

Judges necessarily have a life of experience that can colour their outlook. This may impact a decision if judges are not conscious of the potential influence of their experiences.

In my case, I had suffered two floods while living in Montreal. In both cases, it was clear to me that this city was at fault for not having cleaned the sewers. During the first flood, there was so much water flowing down the driveway that our garage door was smashed, and the water rushed inside like a tsunami. The water in our basement kept rising and eventually covered half the height of the walls. It ruined our furniture, the carpet, and everything that was on the floor. The walls had to be redone, including the Gyproc, plaster, and paint. In addition, the carpet and furniture had to be replaced. Worst of all, I had planned to hang some of my mother's artwork in our basement. Her portfolio was affected by water damage, and much of her work was destroyed. It could not be replaced. All of my diplomas and my degrees were also destroyed. Needless to say, I was upset.

My husband and I saw city trucks cleaning the sewers on our street the day after the flooding, but, by then, it was too late. I instituted a lawsuit against the city. After completely renovating the basement, we suffered another flood. There was less to destroy this time, but the experience was nevertheless traumatic.

When cases dealing with water infiltration and damages arose, I did not need much in the way of explanation. I had lived through the horror, twice. More importantly, I was angry with the city of Montreal, which I considered responsible but which was reluctant to settle with me. I decided that I was not impartial in any case involving the city administration, and it was no longer appropriate for me to sit on any case in which the city was a party.

Other aspects of judges' life experiences also may colour their view of the evidence that they hear. For instance, in a claim I heard against an insurance company that refused compensation after a theft, the company explained that the reason for its refusal to compensate was that the insured had exaggerated his claim. The insurance company presented a number of facts to substantiate its position, including the fact that the insured had listed five television sets among the items stolen from his home. The insurance company pointed to this as proof of an outrageous claim. As the evidence was being presented, I began to list in my mind where the televisions in our home were located. In doing this, I counted five of them. Clearly, while it is not common to have that many televisions in a home, it is not such an exaggeration to own so many television sets.

My life experience also included major home renovations. I found many contractors did work that was shoddy and completely unacceptable: showers that did not drain properly, plumbing that leaked to another floor, tiles that rose and cracked, and so on. When I heard construction cases, I had to put aside my extremely high standards of expected perfection from a service provider and examine the work with as objective an eye as possible. I was always aware of the fact that, in my personal life, I had high expectations of everyone doing a job, irrespective of their profession or occupation, and that I had to temper my expectations to conform to reality. I trust that others on the bench had the same approach.

USING WHAT I KNOW

While experience from life may influence decision making, it goes the other way as well: experience in court can impact on numerous situations in everyday life. The knowledge that I acquired after sitting as a judge in the Civil Division of the Court of Quebec has been useful for me in so many respects. After hearing numerous construction cases, I often felt as if I could construct a house by myself. Even if that was not literally the case, I did gain a great deal of knowledge about a variety of subjects involved in the cases I heard that I would not normally know.

Because of the many renovation cases I had presided over, I was able to caution a friend to see the entire marble slab before buying marble tiles in order to have a uniform pattern; about having the hole for the faucet made in the granite before the counter was installed in her home so that it did not break at its most vulnerable point; about obtaining a written contract regarding the work to be done because otherwise she would be dealing with a "he said, she said" situation if something went wrong; about specifying the payment schedule during the construction or renovation process; about foreseeing a penalty clause if the work was delayed beyond a certain date; and so on.

I was also able to provide advice to friends and family to get an estimate before having a car repaired and how to handle hidden defects when purchasing a home. I constantly encouraged friends to note the name of the representative they had spoken to in any customer service situation and to confirm all conversations in writing. I warned them about the necessity of reading contracts before blindly signing them on the dotted line. I often provided friends with information about the *Consumer Protection Act* and advised them as to what protections were available to them if they purchased a product, and it turned out to be defective.[1]

The knowledge I gained during my career was also of use to me personally. When I purchased a home and had the landfill tested for pyrite,[2] I was not concerned when I received the results. I knew from expert reports I had received in my court cases that the level of pyrite under the house was at an acceptable level. I also knew that pyrite reached its maximum potential for damage in approximately thirty years. Since the house we planned to purchase was older than that, there was little danger the existing percentage of pyrite would eventually increase or that it would cause cracks in the property.

When I was at a hospital for an operation, I recalled one of my cases where the nature of the surgery had not been properly explained. Before signing a consent form in the hospital that stated that I had been informed of the nature of the intervention and the risks associated with it, I asked for and obtained a detailed list of what would happen during the surgery as well as what could possibly go wrong. I knew that I was entitled to know exactly what was envisaged in terms of the intervention

---

Chapter 9

1 *Consumer Protection Act*, CQLR c P-40.1.

2 Pyrite is a common mineral present in some landfills. When in contact with moisture and air, a chemical reaction takes place causing the crystals in the pyrite to expand. Large amounts of pyrite present in landfills can result in cracks in floors and in walls.

and what possibilities existed in terms of complications. Even though I was reassured that the operation would go smoothly, I scribbled out a will just before I left for the operating room.

ACTIVITIES AND ONGOING ISSUES

I have mentioned that the life of a judge is a busy one. On top of our duties in the courtroom, there were often activities for judges that were connected with our work but did not take place at the courthouse. Judges are expected to keep up to date with the law as well as current affairs, and there were many courses offered to me by the court during my years on the bench. They ranged from specific courses on civil law or courses for those in the Criminal Division or the Youth Court to courses that simply enhanced our general knowledge.

I took a number of courses, some of which were incredibly interesting, while others were not very useful. The courses I took on legal research skills, for instance, were not of any help. The course was given to a relatively large group of judges, and there was no possibility of a personal explanation at any point. If I did not understand one concept, it was impossible to follow the remainder of the concepts since the approach was akin to building blocks. One needed to understand step one in order to follow step two or three. I fell behind and was unable to follow the remainder of the course.

In addition, the spelling mistakes I invariably made in written French rendered electronic research useless. If I spelled a word incorrectly, or if I so much as forgot an accent, I would find that there were no matches for my search. I took the same research course twice, and, after not mastering the research methods either time, I gave up and found a more user-friendly site where I could do my research. However, it usually generated hundreds, if not thousands, of decisions, and these were not necessarily specific enough to meet my needs. Luckily, I had a great relationship with our legal department. Most of the time, I simply asked them to find the decisions I required, and they were happy to oblige.

The course on how to better write judgments and to deliver them from the bench was much more helpful. We were given a hypothetical case and were required to render a judgment immediately after hearing the evidence. I was excellent at the written aspect of the course and was surprised to learn that I also excelled at presenting an oral judgment. However, despite the skills I acquired in that training course, when I was back in court, I rarely rendered my judgments from the bench. I preferred reviewing my notes from a hearing and rendering my decisions only after they were drafted. This way, I had time to think about the evidence and ensure that I was totally comfortable with my decision.

One of the courses I appreciated the most was called social realities. Part of it dealt with current events, and, at the time, I wondered why such material would be presented to judges. I assumed that all judges would be aware of current affairs given that we should keep up to date with the news around us. However, another aspect of the course was a lecture on the Islamic religion. My knowledge in this area was limited, and I found the course interesting. What struck me most was how many aspects of orthodox Judaism and Islam were very similar, if not the very same, and were both so far removed from my practice of reform Judaism, which is very liberal and modern.

In addition to courses that were offered to judges on a voluntary basis, we were all required to attend two days of mandatory training every spring. These courses were given by lawyers, other judges, or law professors who were specialists in a particular field of law. The courses dealt with various aspects of civil law, criminal law, and youth protection, and we attended the courses that were applicable to the division in which we sat. Most often, the courses concerned changes in legislation that had been enacted since our previous training session. Courses were also given to bring us up to date on case law or developments that had taken place in a specific area of law.

The sessions were intense. We were in the classroom from early morning until the end of the day, and discussions were encouraged. It gave us the opportunity to debate particular subjects among ourselves, particularly when the case law was divided and there was not a consensus among us regarding an issue. The discussions also allowed us to try to arrive at a consensus on a contentious subject, although, most often, it was the Court of Appeal that determined the approach to take on a divided issue. In general, these sessions were enlightening as well as necessary. They enabled us to stay current in our knowledge and aware of any changes in the state of the law in all the areas we would be hearing.

CONFERENCES AND PARTYING

In addition to the courses that we took, an annual conference was held in the fall of every year in a different location in the province of Quebec for all the judges of the Court of Quebec. It was part training and part socialization. Since the judges are scattered throughout the entire province, the conference was an occasion for all of us to get together for a few days in a relaxed atmosphere and catch up. There were, and still are, approximately three hundred judges on the Court of Quebec, and there were many judges I didn't know. Judges who were friendly with each other got together for lunches and dinners during the conference, but judges from different districts often joined us. The conferences gave us all a chance to meet judges from other parts of the province.

I usually travelled to our annual conferences with my friend and colleague Juanita Westmoreland. Since we sat in different divisions of the court, we did not see each other very often during the judicial year. Driving to the conference gave us a chance to get together and talk about what had been happening in our lives. The only problem in travelling together was that neither of us had any sense of direction. It did not matter whether I was driving and Juanita was navigating or she was driving and I was navigating. We consistently got lost and arrived at our destination hours after our scheduled arrival.

On one trip, we actually drove into Quebec City, where the conference was being held, but did not realize where we were. We continued our journey and, sometime later, found that we had left the city far behind. From then on, we always gave ourselves plenty of time for our trips. We often laugh about our driving adventures. Recently, we travelled to visit a common friend who lives out of town, but, this time, we had a GPS. For the first time, we had no trouble finding her house and arrived exactly at the scheduled time.

My favourite site for our conferences was Quebec City. We often stayed at the well-known Chateau Frontenac Hotel as it was off-season, and the rates were reasonable.

It was like a mini holiday. We were able to visit art galleries, museums, eat in the excellent restaurants that the city has to offer, and wander through the many attractive shops during our stay. Most judges were joined by their spouses or partners who were invited to accompany us for the activities that were organized in the evenings. The conferences were generally much less intense than our spring training sessions. Nevertheless, they were focused on a particular subject, with speakers and panel discussions. Conference subjects ranged from recent case law of the Supreme Court of Canada to the use of the internet in our work and in our research.

The conferences ended every year with a gala dinner dance. The dress code was formal wear; everyone and their spouses got dressed to the nines. Dinner was elaborate, and the music was lively. At first, I found it rather amusing to see my colleagues, who were for the most part rather staid and conservative, dancing so energetically throughout the evening. The festivities always continued well into the night with an open bar in one of the hotel rooms. It was a party like most parties. People drank, mingled, and partied until the morning hours. No one talked about law at these get-togethers.

Chapter 10

Credibility

In every trial, the parties present their version of the facts. Very often, they contradict each other. In addition, a party or a witness can contradict himself when presenting the facts of a case. When parties present diametrically contradictory facts, we refer to the case as "he says, she says."

One of the greatest challenges for a judge is determining who is telling the truth and which version is the correct one. In some cases, the decision is clear. However, in others, it is not evident which party is presenting an accurate version of what transpired. Thankfully, when it is not possible to reach a conclusion, the *Civil Code* provides the necessary solution.[1] The cases described in this chapter give an idea of the difficulties involved in deciding who is right, whether in a regular civil law case, cases falling under the *Highway Safety Code*, or cases coming under legislation governing health and safety.[2]

ARE THEY LYING?

One of my colleagues boldly told me that it was easy to tell when someone was lying and lacked credibility. We were

---

Chapter 10

1 *Civil Code of Québec*, CQLR c CCQ-1991.

2 *Highway Safety Code*, CQLR c C-24.2.

on our way to a meeting, and I regret that I did not have the opportunity to ask how she was able to determine with such certainty whether a party or a witness was telling the truth. For me, this was far from evident, and I am sure that most of my fellow colleagues would agree with me.

Many witnesses have difficulty relating their version of the facts. Basically, they are uncomfortable being in a courtroom, which is an unfamiliar setting. For the most part, they are nervous when they are called upon to testify in court. They speak too quickly; they stumble over their testimony; and, because of their lack of composure and their speech, they often do not appear to be telling the truth. On the other hand, some people can lie with ease. They can provide a story that is completely false without any visible signs of their lack of truthfulness or misrepresentation.

So, then, how does a judge tell the difference between the truth and lies? It is not easy. Essentially, we look to the credibility of the witness. Has the individual presented a number of facts and, then, in cross examination by the opposing lawyer, admitted to a contrary version of the facts? Has the individual claimed that something took place at a given date and later in his testimony provided another timeline?

In one case, the witness explained their reaction to an event, saying: "*Mes bras tombaient*" (my arms dropped). He explained that he was totally surprised and stunned. Then, sometime later in his testimony, describing a different event, he repeated that he was so surprised that his arms dropped. The third time that he expressed the same phrase, I was no longer taken by his surprise. I had surmised that it was simply an expression of speech that he used. Consequently, it had no value in substantiating his testimony about the first event, which he claimed had such a large impact on him.

Generally, contradictions in the witness's testimony, a lack of transparency in providing information, evasive answers, improbable scenarios, and claims by the witness that he does not recall events that should be easily recalled tend to raise doubts about the credibility of the witness. However, even such criteria can be misleading. I was a witness in a case many years ago. My significant other at the time was detained at the airport on his way home from a trip; it later turned out that he had the same family name as another person who was wanted for fraud, and he was erroneously flagged for detention. After waiting a considerable period of time, I told the officials that I was his lawyer and asked to see him. The confusion was finally sorted out, but, nevertheless, there remained an issue: he had an outstanding traffic ticket from many years before. In order to avoid arrest, he was escorted by police officers to the nearest police station to pay the ticket. I followed them in my own car. Because of his detention at the airport, he sued the government.

At the trial, I testified as to the time of day that I arrived at the airport, the lengthy delay that ensued, and the actions I took on his behalf. I had vivid recall of what transpired at the airport, and I also had a visual memory of what my significant other was wearing. But when I was asked in cross-examination what took place when we left the airport, I replied that we headed for home. I completely forgot that he had left in a police car to go and pay his traffic ticket. Because I had appeared to be so certain about a number of facts but had failed to recall other facts in a continuous timeline, the court discarded my testimony, concluding that I lacked credibility. I was shocked.

However, the event served to remind me that missing information in testimony is not necessarily a sign that the witness is unreliable; rather, it may just be the manifestation of stress.

LIFTING A CAR SEIZURE

Often parties provide explanations that are simply not believable, and they clearly lack credibility. One area where such testimony occurred frequently when I was on the bench was in cases involving requests to lift car seizures. If the owner of a vehicle is found driving the car while his licence has been cancelled or suspended, a police officer can immediately seize and impound the vehicle for thirty days. To recover the vehicle before the thirty days are over, the owner must present a motion to the Court of Quebec and convince a judge that they were not aware that they were disqualified from driving.

The same principle applies if someone whose licence was cancelled or suspended is driving the owner's vehicle. The owner of the vehicle must establish that he was unaware that the person who drove his vehicle was disqualified or did not hold a proper licence. It is not sufficient to say that he did not know the status of the person's licence; he has to show that he made a reasonable attempt to verify the relevant information. Alternatively, the owner must prove that he had not consented to the driver using the vehicle.

The typical explanations that I heard in these cases were that the applicants had never received the notice from the Automobile Insurance Association advising them that their licence had been revoked, although they had not moved and seemed to have received every other notice and piece of mail delivered to their home. Other excuses included the claim that their mother picked up their notice and did not give it to them; that they had separated from their girlfriend or boyfriend and their significant other must have thrown out the notice; that their neighbours sometimes took their mail; that their mail delivery was not very reliable; and, finally, one applicant who actually claimed that his dog ate the notice.

The explanations given when someone else was driving the owner's car were just as numerous, and most often lacked any credibility. They included such excuses as their son took their keys without their knowledge after finding the keys in a drawer where they were always kept; that the keys were stolen by their son or daughter from their purse while they were sleeping; that their keys were missing and they did not realize it; and so on.

Of course, when they lent their car to someone else, everyone assured me that they had verified the status of that person's driving licence. "How did you check?" I would ask. The typical reply I received from the owner was that he asked the person who would be driving his car whether he had a valid licence. However, this does not constitute a proper verification. Invariably, everyone claimed that they needed their car to get to work or to pick up their child from daycare. Unfortunately, that was not a sufficient motive to have the seizure lifted, nor was the fact that they had paid an outstanding traffic ticket immediately after the car was seized. For the payment to be valid, the ticket had to have been paid before the seizure took place.

I recall several arguments that took place between couples in the courtroom when I refused to lift the seizure because the reason that was given was not valid in law. In many cases, I felt badly for the rejected applicants since I could imagine how inconvenient it was for someone to be deprived of their car for a period as long as a month. However, unless the excuse was one foreseen by the *Highway Safety Act* and was also convincing, it remained what it was: simply an excuse.

THE RESTRICTED DRIVER'S LICENCE

Judges of the Court of Quebec also have jurisdiction to issue a restricted driver's licence to a person whose licence has been cancelled because of too many demerit points. To obtain the restricted licence, the person must prove to the judge that he must drive a road vehicle to carry on his principal means of earning a livelihood. The necessary evidence is not difficult to obtain. The only document an individual has to submit is a letter from the applicant's employer that confirms the nature of his employment, working hours, and the need to drive a vehicle for the purposes of his employment. A restricted driver's licence is not granted simply to travel to an employee's workplace; it is only granted when a vehicle is needed for the employee to actually do his job.

Some judges, in issuing a restricted licence, indicate the days and the hours during which the individual can drive a vehicle, which correspond to their working hours. Others simply indicate the person's occupation and the fact that the licence is restricted and issued for the purpose of carrying out the individual's job. For my part, I would explain in court that the restricted licence was not to go to movies, restaurants, or visit friends but was only to be used for work. If the individual who was granted such a licence was caught driving for other purposes, they would be subject to more severe sanctions.

A person who works as a taxi driver, a delivery person, a bus driver, or a truck driver clearly needs a restricted driver's licence to be able to work. Other occupations that require the employee to drive a vehicle for work and who need a restricted licence to do so include an ambulance driver, a chauffeur, and a driving instructor. This is also the case for people who travel from one location to another to meet with clients at their homes or offices, such as service providers or marketing representatives. The same, however, is not true for many other occupations or professions.

In one case that I heard, the applicant, who was a pharmacist, testified that she needed a restricted licence to get to her pharmacy. She claimed that she could be called to go in on a consultation even on the weekends when she was at her country home, which was about an hour and a half outside the city. In essence, she was attempting to circumvent the system and be able to use her car at all times, not only for work but also to go back and forth to her second residence. I dismissed the application. Other cases involved people who maintained that they needed a restricted licence for various reasons to carry out their work when, in fact, they simply needed to have a car to reach their workplace.

It was truly fascinating to hear how many people claimed they had to work seven days a week or were on call 24/7, even though they were not taxi drivers, bus drivers, travelling service providers, or the like. Their testimony was simply not credible.

THE LONG-DISTANCE DRIVER

You may be surprised to know how often the lack of credibility on the part of one or the other party or witnesses arises. In some cases, I reached a conclusion about the lack of credibility because of contradictions in the testimony I heard, while, in other cases, the story that was presented, while consistent, was simply not believable. One such case involved a long-distance driver who was fired when he failed to make his delivery within the time frame set by his employer.

The *Canada Labour Code* foresees that an employee may refuse to perform work when he has reasonable cause to believe that the work he is refusing to do constitutes a danger to himself or to another employee.[3] In this case, the long-distance truck driver refused to continue driving because he had exhausted the maximum number of hours he was permitted to work in an eight-hour driving cycle. He was immediately dismissed. He stated that he was not only fired but also abandoned at a truck stop in the United States. He had no money and had to call a labour relations officer in Ottawa to assist him in returning to Canada.

The employer claimed that the employee in question had voluntarily quit and had abandoned his truck in the United States. I found it inconceivable that the employee voluntarily left his job while in the United States with no funds and no means of returning home. The employee's explanation for not driving any further was related to safety considerations and was more plausible than that of the employer. The employer then attempted to show the employee as incompetent but failed to substantiate its claim.

I concluded that the employee was terminated because of his refusal to work, and his refusal was justified based on the provisions of the *Labour Code*. I ordered that the employee be reinstated and compensated for his losses.

---

3 *Canada Labour Code*, RSC 1985, c L-2.

DECIDING THE OUTCOME

Though the law specifies what rules apply to an issue, it does not determine how a case should be decided. The outcome depends not only on the law but also on the evidence. In many cases, judges have a certain amount of discretion. For example, an employer who dismisses an employee must give him reasonable notice. When notice is not given, the employee is entitled to compensation equivalent to the period of reasonable notice. However, the *Civil Code* does not specify what constitutes reasonable notice.

The amount of notice that is required depends on a number of factors that have been elaborated in our case law, such as the age of the employee, his position in the hierarchy, his salary level, the length of service, his responsibilities, the length of time involved to find another job, and so on. These factors are guidelines. Ultimately, a judge has discretion.

The area in which judges exercise the most discretion is often in awarding damages. Parties seek damages not only for physical injuries or material damage but also for trouble and inconvenience and for moral damages in the case of psychological distress. Parties usually ask for as much compensation as possible, knowing that a judge cannot award more than the amount sought. They hope that, by asking for a large award, they will obtain an adequate amount. Very often, however, this only means that the amounts claimed are exaggerated and are considerably reduced by the courts.

I often awarded plaintiffs less than they were asking for because lawyers are not realistic! Other times, it was a result of the complexities of the case. As an example, in one case, I awarded considerably less compensation than the plaintiffs claimed when a contractor damaged their property, although I had found the contractor to be responsible. Part of the reduced amount of compensation resulted from the delay in instituting the lawsuit, such that a portion of the claim was out of time. I also concluded that the plaintiffs should share in the responsibility for the damages since they had failed to take any measures to protect their grounds despite the fact that the contractor had dumped snow on them in previous years.

In my discretion, I granted part of their claim for loss of enjoyment and quality of life, but I denied their request for damages for an alleged abuse of procedure. The couple sought $50,000, plus costs for abuse of procedure. I awarded them $10,500.

HE SAYS—SHE SAYS

In most cases, the law is clear, but the facts presented are not. For instance, take the case where the buyers of a home sue the seller for defects that they discovered after moving into their home. I heard many of these cases in my tenure. An essential element that the buyers must prove to succeed in their case is to establish that the defect in the house they purchased was hidden at the time of sale. The buyers will necessarily claim that the defect was not visible. The sellers, on the other hand, will maintain that the defect was apparent and should have been obvious to any prudent buyer. The outcome of such a case depends on which party the judge believes. This is called a "he says, she says" case.

When there are contradictions in the testimony between the two parties, the legal outcome that emerges depends on which party is deemed credible. An example of "he says, she says" is a case where money has been exchanged between two parties. The plaintiff in such cases seeks the repayment of the money the plaintiff gave to the other party, claiming it was a loan. The defendant claims that it was a gift and that he does not have to repay it. The judge hearing the case is left to decide who is telling the truth.

One case of this nature I heard was a love story without a happy ending. Ben, a dapper elderly man, met Xia and began a relationship. Xia was dissatisfied with her job, where she was earning very little, and decided to quit. Ben initially lent her one thousand dollars, which was to be repaid when she began to work again. After that, Ben told her that he had enough money to share; he continued to provide her with money on a monthly basis. Xia did not find satisfactory employment, and Ben maintained his payments, giving her a one-thousand-dollar cheque each month until the couple had a falling out. During their relationship, Ben gave Xia numerous gifts, including expensive clothes, meals at restaurants, and trips. He also gave her money to purchase a car.

A few years later, their relationship ended, and Ben claimed the reimbursement of the money he had given her—not just the initial one thousand dollars but every cent he had spent on her. Xia denied that the money was a loan and maintained that Ben had told her he would support her; the question of reimbursement had never been discussed. She claimed that Ben had sent her letters, notes, and poetry in which he expressed the love and care he had for her. His feelings were reciprocated by Xia, who expressed similar feelings toward Ben. There had clearly been a warm and affectionate bond between the two. Ben claimed the cheques he had given Xia were periodic loans to be repaid, but there was no inscription on the cheques or any mention as to the parties' intentions. They could be compatible with the claim of a loan; they could equally be compatible with a gift.

This case is an example where it was not clear which party was telling the truth or which version of events was more probable. In such instances, the solution was provided for me by the *Civil Code of Québec*. It states that the person making the claim has the burden of proof. Therefore, when both parties appear to be credible and it is not possible to tell which one is telling the truth, the plaintiff has not met his burden of proof, and his claim will be rejected. While most judges would prefer to reach their own assessment of the evidence, this rule provides a solution to such problematic cases.

In the case of Ben and Xia, I adopted this solution and stated that both parties were credible and consistent in their testimony. Therefore, given the contradictory evidence, the plaintiff (Ben) had not met his burden of proof. As a result, his lawsuit was dismissed.

Chapter 11

Finding Fairness

As my younger brothers and I were growing up, we were taught many values: to be honest and ethical, to act fairly, to have respect for others, and to be open to new or different ideas. When we complained about treatment from our parents on any number of issues, my mother would say: "Well, life's not fair." I always thought it was a strange thing for her to say since we had been brought up to act toward others in a way that was fair. Surely, I thought, life should be fair. If it was not, it was our job to make it as equitable as we could. This attitude served me well as both a lawyer and a judge. But, on occasion, I was forced to confront situations where, no matter what I did, I could not make the outcome "fair."

A case in point took place while I was in law school. At the end of our exams, our marks were posted on the wall. They were supposed to be anonymous; instead of using our names, we were listed by our birth dates. Unfortunately, since I had returned to school after pursuing another career and was much older than the other students, my marks were very public. Before I even saw the posted marks, my classmates would tell me how I had done on a particular exam. I was thankful that my marks were always extremely good. I considered this method of posting our results to be incredibly unjust since my marks were never anonymous. Of course, there was nothing I could do to change the system.

In my legal career, I would sometimes have to confront other unfair situations. Sometimes, I was able to find my path to a fair and just resolution. Other times, my hands were tied by the letter of the law, and there was nothing I could do.

WHEN TWO OUTCOMES ARE POSSIBLE

After hearing a case, reviewing case law, and considering the evidence, I would decide the outcome of the litigation. Since the lawyers had presented evidence and pleaded opposite positions, there are often two possible outcomes. The judge chooses the one that best corresponds with the evidence and the law. But there are times when the outcome is far from evident.

One case that comes to mind is that of an insurance claim. The plaintiffs sued their insurance company after it refused to reimburse the total amount they had paid for a rental car during the repair of their vehicle, which had been badly damaged and required several months to be repaired. At issue was the cost of adding an additional driver to the rental agreement. The problem was that, while the plaintiffs had indicated there would be two people driving the car, they had failed to inform the insurance company that there was an additional charge for that second driver. The insurance company determined the maximum amount it would pay for a comparable substitute vehicle, for the duration of the repair period, based on the cost of a single driver. It refused to pay the extra costs charged by the rental company for having another driver added to the contract. The insurance company based its position on the fact that these charges had not been reported to it when the rental contract was signed.

The clause in the insurance contract was not clear, and I was undecided. I actually wrote two versions of the judgment, one in which the plaintiffs were granted total reimbursement and another in which their claim was rejected. While it was unusual for me to draft two different outcomes, I did so in cases such as this when I considered that the judgment could go either way. I believed that writing two opposing judgments would help me to reach a decision as I would see which one was more compelling. In this case, however, it did not work. I was still stuck.

I decided to consult one of my colleagues. She was not in her office, so I left her secretary a note to give to her. I briefly outlined the facts of the case and included the pertinent clause in the insurance contract. I then went out to lunch with another colleague. During our meal, I talked about my case and the ambiguous clause in the contract, seeking his opinion. He immediately concluded that the insurance policy allowed for the rental of an alternate comparable vehicle for both plaintiffs, with no fee restriction, and, therefore, the insurance company was obliged to cover the costs incurred. According to him, it was immaterial that the insurer had not been informed as to the extra costs.

When I returned to my office, I found the note that I had written to my colleague before lunch, with her comments on it. She concluded that the insurance company had undertaken to pay the plaintiffs the cost of an alternative comparable car but not any additional costs, particularly when it was not aware of such extra costs. She stated categorically that the insurance company, by paying the cost of the rental car, had respected its contractual obligations and was not obliged to cover the extra costs incurred. This left me with a dilemma. It was clear, from a legal standpoint, that either conclusion was acceptable.

I opted for the opinion I had received in writing from my colleague, who had concluded that the insurance company had respected its contractual obligations. I based my decision on the principle that the plaintiffs had the burden of proof. As we say in law, they had to establish their case by "a preponderance of evidence." In other words, in order to succeed, the evidence the plaintiffs presented had to be more credible than that of the insurance company. Since they had not convinced me to render judgment in their favour, I ultimately ruled against them and rejected their claim. I also took into consideration the fact that requiring the insurance company to provide compensation in a case where it had not undertaken to cover any added costs was not fair.

There are no courts of equity in Canada. We are governed by law, not by equity or fairness.[1] However, while we judge with the law in mind, we also try to be just. I heard a number of cases where the decision could easily go one way or the other, but I considered one of the possible solutions to be fairer than the other. Two cases come to mind which illustrate my attempt at finding fairness.

Chapter 11

1 Bryan A Garner, ed, *Black's Law Dictionary*, 7th ed (St Paul, MN: West Group, 1999). The definitions of equity include the following: "(1) Fairness . . . (2) The body of principles constituting what is fair and right. . . . (3) The recourse to principles of justice to correct or supplement the law as applied to particular circumstances."

EMPLOYMENT WITH A GROUP OF COMPANIES

In one case, the plaintiff was approached by an individual who was a consultant for an organization made up of several companies, and he asked the plaintiff to come to work for them as a sales director. The plaintiff was gainfully employed and refused the job offer. He was approached again, this time to work as director general of the organization. This time, the plaintiff accepted. He negotiated a clause in his contract that stipulated that, in the case his job ended, he would be given notice of six months.[2] He also required that the president of the organization sign his contract before he resigned from his employment. He wanted the security of an acknowledgement that he would be part of the entire organization, not just a single company within the group.

The plaintiff began working in his new position. He tried to improve the performance not only of one of the companies where he worked most directly but also of the organization as a whole. In this context, he was provided with the financial results of each of the related companies at organizational meetings. A short time after he began work, the plaintiff was advised that he was being laid off because of a reorganization of operations. He was told that the company he worked for no longer existed. The plaintiff asked to be relocated to another part of the organization, but he was unsuccessful. He finally left the organization and found another job, albeit at a lesser salary. He sued the organization for the six months' salary he had negotiated as well as his commissions, insurance coverage, and other benefits.

2 Today, the amount of notice would be considerably longer for a person holding a senior position in a company.

The defence tried to show that the plaintiff had contracted his employment with only one of the companies and not with the larger organization. If this was true, it would result in the dismissal of the plaintiff's case. It appeared to me to be completely unjust, especially considering that the plaintiff had been specifically told that the available position was that of director general for the organization.

I asked our legal department to assist me. Were there any other cases of a similar nature, where a set of circumstances led the party in question to believe that he was dealing with an organization rather than a single company within a larger organization? I knew the outcome I wanted for the case—I wanted a fair result for the plaintiff. However, my decision had to have a legal basis; I could not simply opt for a solution that I considered to be "just." Our legal department found a very similar case with an outcome that was equitable. This was exactly the type of judgment I needed.

An analysis of the evidence in my case showed that the various facts that the consultant had presented to the plaintiff led the plaintiff to believe that he had been employed by the organization as a whole rather than by only one of the companies. The announcement in the newspaper regarding the position also referred to the organization as the hiring body. Even though the company that had hired the plaintiff and the greater organization were legally distinct, their commercial activities were of the same nature and were intertwined. The same person was the president and majority shareholder of both entities. There was an exchange of financial information, meetings, employees, and management between the companies and the central organization. All the facts pointed to the plaintiff's position as being part of a structured organization. While the head of the organization could have specified that the position offered to the plaintiff was not part of the overall organization, he did not do so.

I concluded that the defendant's actions were fraudulent and granted the compensation sought by the plaintiff. For me, it was an equitable conclusion and one with a strong legal basis. However, the defendant appealed my judgment. If I had any doubts about the decision that I had rendered, it was put to rest by the Court of Appeal, which upheld my judgment. I was rather pleased with the outcome of the case.

COMMISSION FOR A RENTAL PROPERTY

Another case that comes to mind concerns a claim put forward by a real estate broker for his commission. The broker had received a mandate from a client, ABC, to rent out its premises. The broker found Company X, which wished to rent the space from ABC. The broker's contract stated that he would receive a commission from ABC for renting their premises and for renting any additional space during the term of the lease as well as for a successful lease renewal. However, the contract was not clear as to whether the commission was payable for only the first renewal or for many periods of renewal.

The tenant, Company X, decided to renew its lease with ABC at the end of the term. It did so with the help of the broker. ABC paid a commission to the broker in accordance with its contract. ABC considered that it had met its obligations to the broker and owed no further payment.

Before the next renewal period, Company X decided to continue to rent premises from ABC but wanted to modify the conditions of its lease. In addition to arranging for a different term, it enlarged the existing space, added space from another floor, obtained extra parking, created a rooftop terrace, included new costs, and so on. This time, however, Company X did not contact the broker but proceeded to negotiate the terms of the lease on its own. Company X subsequently advised the broker that it was remaining in the premises and had concluded a lease with ABC. The broker sent an invoice to ABC for his commission. ABC refused to pay, arguing that it had negotiated with Company X on its own and that the broker had not been involved in any way. The broker then sued, claiming his commission.

The outcome of this case depended on the interpretation to be given to the clauses of the contract with the broker and, in particular, whether a commission was payable for each and every renewal of the lease. ABC and Company X both considered that the contract was clear: a commission was payable for only one renewal. The broker interpreted the contract differently. In such cases, according to the rules of interpretation, the court must determine what the original intention of the parties was. In addition, the interpretation must favour an equitable result and a reasonable commercial result.

I analyzed the contract and determined that ABC and Company X understood that the broker would be compensated for his initial work of finding a tenant and for his intervention in a single renewal. ABC had already paid a significant commission in accordance with its contract and had respected its obligations. Having determined the intention of the parties, I could have ended the case with this conclusion. However, the broker maintained that he was entitled to a commission for every renewal of the lease.

In order to succeed, the broker had to establish that the last lease was a renewal of the original lease. I concluded that it was not a renewal. Taking into consideration all the changes to the lease that had been negotiated, it was a very distinct agreement. Moreover, the broker was not responsible for the major changes in the space and rental conditions. Therefore, I dismissed the lawsuit; I held that the broker did not have the right to a commission.

While I firmly felt it was not equitable to award compensation to someone who was in no way involved in the negotiations or in drafting the lease, I felt more comfortable in my decision, which was based on the rules of interpretation. The principles of interpretation that seek the intention of the parties and the more reasonable commercial result allowed me to adopt a conclusion that I believed brought about an equitable result.

MY HANDS WERE TIED

Most of the time, judges can draft a judgment that corresponds with the facts of the case, the law, and with what appears to be a sound and fair decision. Exceptionally, there were times when the required outcome appeared to me to be unfair, but there was little I could do. This was the situation in a file concerning an appeal by the public curator against a decision rendered by the Access to Information Commission.

In essence, a woman who I will call Ms. M. wanted to rectify a document found in her mother's file, which was held by the public curator. Specifically, there was a note on file that stated that Ms. M. was forbidden by a court order to visit her mother because of Ms. M.'s previous physical violence. According to Ms. M., this information was false, and she wanted it removed from her mother's file. The public curator refused her request. Ms. M. then asked the Access to Information Commission to revise the public curator's refusal to rectify her mother's file. The public curator objected. It claimed the concerned information was in a file, which was under the public curator's responsibility, and that the Access to Information Commission did not have jurisdiction to hear the request to revise the public curator's decision.

In the appeal, I had to decide on the competence of the Access to Information Commission. After a detailed analysis of the law, it was clear that all files held by the public curator were confidential. As such, the commission did not have the authority to hear a request to rectify the information contained in these files. While the law was clear, what also was clear to me was that there was a void. The law governing the public curator did not provide any means of rectifying a file; it was silent in that respect. I concluded that it was up to the legislator to fill this void and not the courts. I could not provide Ms. M. with the possibility of changing the contents of her mother's file.

The problem I had was that the police report that M. submitted in evidence showed that Ms. M. was correct in her assertions. According to the police report, Ms. M. had never been mentioned in any court order. She had no criminal record and was not violent. An error had occurred; it was another person who was the subject of the court order, not Ms. M. Ms. M. desperately wanted to correct the error in her mother's file in order to clear her name.

As already indicated, the law did not provide me with the possibility of granting her what she sought. However, I attempted to rectify the erroneous entry in the mother's file another way, by writing an *obiter dictum*[3] in which I reproduced the police report. I did this because I understood how important it was for Ms. M. to establish that she had not done anything wrong. Even though she was unable to change the contents of her mother's file, she nevertheless had a judgment that reprinted the police report and that clearly indicated that the allegation against Ms. M. in her mother's file, held by the public curator, was unfounded. I felt that, although my hands were tied and I could not by law specifically provide the outcome Ms. M. wanted, at the very least, I could publicly recognize her innocence in a matter that was, for her, so very important.

TAX EVASION

Taxes are payable by virtually every citizen. Some people operating businesses attempt to avoid paying their share. Clearly, such behaviour is against the law. It is also unfair to society. While most contracts are written, it is not unusual for parties to conclude contracts verbally. A verbal contract is legally valid; the problem is often proving what was agreed upon when there is a dispute between the parties. Often, however, when parties conclude verbal contracts, they do so in order for the work or services to be paid in cash in order to avoid paying taxes for the service. The Court of Quebec hears many such cases. A maxim that is frequently cited is "*frustra legis auxilium quaerit qui in legem*

3 An *obiter dictum* is a judicial comment made in delivering a judicial opinion or a comment made by a judge in a judgment that is not necessary to the decision in the case and therefore cannot be used as a precedent. It can be said to be a remark made or an opinion expressed by a judge in his decision that is not directly on the question before the court.

committit"—namely, that if you break the law, you will seek recourse in the law in vain.[4]

In one of the first judgments written in Quebec that dealt with this issue, a mason was claiming money owed for his services. At trial, when he was asked why he had not produced an invoice detailing his work, he admitted that he had not sent the client an invoice because the parties had agreed to make the contract "under the table" in order not to pay taxes. The court considered that such a contract was illegal and was "an absolute nullity."[5] A contract that is null is deemed never to have existed.[6] Since the contract ran contrary to public interest, the court rejected the mason's lawsuit. It held that a court of justice could not sanction a contract between two parties when they had agreed to make a deal that contravened fiscal laws governing this type of transaction.

Subsequently, the court intervened in several other cases where it found that the contract was concluded in violation of fiscal laws. I followed the case law in the files I heard where the contract did not include taxes or where there was a cash transaction without the payment of taxes. I was always surprised that parties were not embarrassed to come before the court when they had committed an illegal act.

However, in one of my cases, the issue of taxes arose even though the contract clearly provided for them. A client had hired a contractor to renovate her property,

---

4 "*Celui qui viole la loi cherche en vain le secours de la loi.*" Albert Mayrand, *Dictionnaire de maxims et locutions latines utilisées en droit*, 3d ed (Cowansville, QC: Éditions Yvon Blais, 1994) at 164.

5 The case was presided over by Judge Guy Gagnon, now a judge of the Court of Appeal of Quebec.

6 *Civil Code of Québec*, CQLR c CCQ-1991, s 1422.

and a written contract was signed. The client ended the contract prematurely, alleging that the work had not been completed and she was dissatisfied with the services. The contractor sued for the balance of its bill, while the client claimed she had paid all that was owed for the work that had been completed.

After evaluating the evidence, I concluded that a certain amount billed was not payable since the contractor had not finished the job and had damaged some wood panelling. After calculating the cost of the project and the reduction I was granting because of the unfinished work and the damages, there remained the sum foreseen as taxes. Despite the fact that the client maintained that she had fully paid any amount owed, she had not satisfied me that she was exempt from paying taxes. As a result, I ordered her to pay the contractor the required taxes and stipulated that the contractor was to remit that amount to the appropriate authorities. I considered that such a decision not only respected fiscal laws but also was fair to society.

Chapter 12

Access to Justice

Access to justice is an ongoing problem in courts all around the world, primarily because it is costly to institute an action or defend against one. So many people can't afford the legal fees involved, which often run into thousands and thousands of dollars. The problem becomes even more acute when the opponent is wealthy or powerful. Another problem in the field of law is that legal jargon, full of archaic language, is so often incomprehensible to lay people. This chapter details these issues and provides examples of cases where I was able to provide access to justice.

AFFORDING JUSTICE

Year after year, at the annual opening of the courts, the same topic was constantly broached: "access to justice." Every year, a discussion took place concerning a serious problem that citizens encountered—namely, not being able to access our justice system.

Committees on our Bar Association have been formed to tackle the problem. Various organizations, such as Justice de Proximité, provide legal information, free of charge, either through individual consultations at its offices or by way of lectures on various subjects that are presented to the public. Other organizations, such as Educaloi, provide information online. The Department of Justice also offers information and videos to assist citizens by featuring various subjects of legal issues. Pamphlets dealing with different topics in a layperson's terms are also available at the courthouse.

Despite all of this, in my view, none of these organizations or documentation truly fills the void. They provide legal information but not legal advice. That does not give the individual concerned with a legal problem any idea whether he has a valid case. If the individual does have a case that has merit and could be litigated, there is not enough information to guide him as to how to proceed, such as what tribunal has jurisdiction, what proceedings are required, what evidence is needed to substantiate a claim or a defence, and so on.

For the very well-off, there is no problem; they can hire the best possible legal counsel in the area of the law they need. The cost will likely be in the thousands of dollars and, in particular cases, over a hundred thousand dollars, but, as the saying goes, "money is no object." For the very poor, there is legal aid. This service tends to specialize in the areas of the greatest need, such as criminal law and family law. When other issues arise, individuals may obtain legal counsel but not necessarily with someone who has expertise in the specific field of law. Some law firms offer pro bono services that are geared toward those who cannot afford regular legal services, but the majority of law firms shy away from such work.

For those who are neither very poor nor very wealthy, the cost of legal services can be prohibitive. Generally, lawyers charge by the hour. The cost varies depending on the law firm and runs from a couple of hundred dollars per hour at the low end to seven hundred dollars or more per hour at the upper end. It does not take much time before the bills run into the tens or hundreds of thousands of dollars, which few people can afford.

While an individual who would like to sue another has the option of proceeding or not after being advised of the cost of litigating, the same is not necessarily true for the defendant. Those who are sued have few options. Either they pay the amount sought in the lawsuit or, if they consider that they are not responsible for the claim against them, they defend themselves. In the latter case, they may find themselves burdened with thousands of dollars of unexpected legal expenses to establish the absence of liability, with no guarantee that they will be successful.

And for those who would like to handle a legal problem on their own, the task can be daunting. It is virtually impossible for someone without a legal background to navigate the legal system, file their own proceedings, and plead their cases on their own. It is only when I have been asked by friends for help with their legal problems, in areas of the law with which I am not familiar, that I have come to realize how problematic it is for a layperson to comprehend what is required and how difficult it is to manoeuvre through a complex system they cannot possibly understand.

I have recommended legal specialists to family and friends in various areas of the law, including medical malpractice, hidden defects, civil responsibility, family law, and rental law. I have explained the law and what is involved in various situations. I have been able to assist friends with their lawsuits in civil, commercial, and employment matters. What was straightforward for me in terms of the law and how to mount a file seemed like a mountain to them. The terminology itself was akin to a foreign language that they did not understand but had to master.

In one particular case when a friend asked for my help in dealing with penal law, I was stumped. Although I had dealt with infractions under a penal code when I was at the Quebec Labour Court, the area that I heard in that court was limited to construction cases in the context of health and safety issues.[1] Our procedures were very straightforward. We did not have a crown prosecutor involved or any of the related procedures that are involved in penal law, and I had never practised in that area as a lawyer.

In the case involving my friend, I was able to do the research and understand what the Crown would try to establish, but I was not familiar with the procedures. I had never attended such a hearing and was not certain whether there was a preliminary inquiry or not, at what point the evidence was divulged, and even whether a postponement could be obtained verbally or whether the request had to be written. I suggested a possible defence to my friend but was not sure that such a defence would be accepted. Even if it was, I had no assurance that it would be effective in obtaining an acquittal. I felt totally inadequate, and my friend was overwhelmed. I can only imagine what it must be like for someone who has no knowledge of the law to try and defend himself without representation. A lawyer would be the appropriate option. However, I learned that the cost of my friend losing her case would amount to a few

---

Chapter 12

1 *Code of Penal Procedure*, CQLR c C-25.1.

hundred dollars, while representation by a lawyer would cost several thousand dollars in legal fees. Given that she was looking at a fine, not jail time, it did not make sense to pay a lawyer when the cost would far exceed the potential penalty to be paid if my friend lost the case. Fortunately for this friend, I contacted a criminal law specialist I knew who agreed to quickly provide her with the necessary explanations and information without any charge.

Personally, I believe the entire legal system is unnecessarily complicated. I have witnessed more than one reform, which has been intended to simplify legal procedures but has made little concrete change. In fact, I have not been at all convinced that any of the changes I have seen over the years actually made it easier to institute a lawsuit or defend oneself from a lawsuit. The rules are still numerous and complex. I often wonder why the law cannot be written in lay terms or why proceedings cannot be such that anyone can present a claim or a defence with ease.

Alternatively, I believe that there should be "legal care" similar to Medicare—that is, when legal services are required, the cost is assumed by the province as it is with medical insurance. Imagine how unfair it is for someone who is erroneously accused of a crime but who has the burden of defending himself? In some countries, such as Norway, the cost of a defence in a criminal trial is covered by the state. I believe we should have a similar system. Unfortunately, we do not have this type of protection in our country.

For civil and commercial lawsuits when the amount involved is small, the Small Claims Court offers the possibility to have a case heard at a minimal cost, and mediations are also available to resolve disputes. Unfortunately, when the amounts involved in litigation are considerable, the Small Claims Court is not available.

The legal profession is very conservative, and changes are slow. Perhaps good access to justice will become a reality someday. However, at present, access still seems as elusive a goal as it ever was, especially when it comes to seeking justice against those with a preponderance of power or privilege.

YOU CAN FIGHT CITY HALL

Even in cases where a party has the means of instituting a lawsuit or defending a lawsuit, there are situations of disproportionate power between the parties, whether it is financial or one of authority. There is a well-known adage that states: "You can't fight city hall." The implication is that the little guy simply cannot fight the big guys, who have more power and more resources. This is not always true, as can be seen in the following case where the "little guy" prevailed over city hall.

A couple living in the suburbs of Montreal had a lovely house surrounded by a picturesque garden. To provide privacy, they planted a double row of cedars on the edge of their property. They prided themselves on the beauty of their plants and particularly their hedge. One winter, they noted that the snow removal services had blown wet and contaminated snow onto their hedge. They advised their city that their hedge had been damaged. They sent photographs to substantiate their claim for damages to replace some of their trees. The city denied responsibility.

In the ensuing years, the snow, salt, and dirt continued to be blown onto their property together with ice pellets. Their cedars, which had been green and healthy, began to deteriorate. Their ornamental shrubs were also damaged by the blown snow and ice pellets. Ultimately, the hedge became so damaged that the couple lost the privacy the hedge had provided. The couple complained to the snow removal crew and to the director of public works on several occasions, but nothing changed. Finally, the couple sued the city, claiming compensation for the damage to their hedge and vegetation.

The city maintained that it had acted with diligence and care in carrying out its operations, but the photographs told a different story; they showed chemical burns, branches covered by snow, broken branches, missing foliage, transparent areas, and plants buried under pellets and ice. The city also maintained that part of the claim was prescribed—that is, it was out of time—since the delays for instituting a lawsuit had expired. In addition, the city claimed that it was not responsible for any prejudice caused by the fault of a contractor to whom it had subcontracted work and, therefore, only the contractor could be held liable.

After evaluating the evidence, I concluded that part of the claim had been presented too late, but a claim could validly be made for the remaining years. As well, I ruled that all the damages could not be attributed solely to the contractor but were the also the result of the city's negligence. In evaluating the damages, I considered the fact that the hedge was extremely important for the couple since the cedars provided a screen and gave the couple privacy on their property. The city's method of evaluating the damages did not provide adequate compensation for the actual loss suffered by the couple.

Finally, I noted that, rather than attempting to resolve a problem with one of its citizens, the city had adopted the adage: "You can't fight city hall." Although the initial claim for damages was for only $16,977.61 and probably could have been settled for less, the city chose to vigorously fight the case; it spent over forty-five thousand dollars on legal fees and expert costs before the trial and presumably a substantial amount for the trial itself. I found all of that to be grossly unreasonable and disproportionate in light of the amount in dispute and the lack of complexity of the case. The couple did not obtain the total amount of compensation they had claimed, but their problem was heard. They were able to show that their claim was valid and that they were at least partially reimbursed. Hopefully, the city would change the way it treated the couple's property so that they could regrow their hedge and regain their privacy.

A LAWYER'S CONFLICT OF INTEREST

Access to justice is not only difficult when an individual is facing a powerful organization or someone in a position of authority but also when a person challenges someone in the legal profession. Lawyers are governed by a *Code of Ethics*, and it is presumed that they will act in good faith.[2] However, this is not always the case. The following story is one of the most glaring examples of bad faith on the part of a lawyer, but justice did prevail.

Before judges retire, we are given several months to complete all our judgments. When I was still a little more than a year away from retirement, I only had a few more months of scheduled hearings. After beginning my final case, I had an accident as well as several unexpected surgeries. As a result, I was absent from work for several months.

I had cases in progress in the regular Civil Division, which still required several days of hearings to complete.

2 *Code of Professional Conduct of Lawyers*, CQLR c B-1, r 3.1.

The choice I was given was to have another judge listen to the recordings of what had transpired and complete the hearings, which would place a tremendous burden on a colleague, or have another judge redo the entire trial, which would be costly and unfair to the litigants. I decided to complete the cases myself during the period when I was no longer required to hear any more cases. It seemed to me to be the only proper way to deal with the situation. However, my final case turned out to be very complex and one of the most difficult cases of my career. It was also a case where a litigant was facing an uphill battle: he was trying to obtain funds he alleged were owed to him by a lawyer and a company. In short, he was seeking justice.

The details of the case are too lengthy and cumbersome to present. In essence, a law firm instituted an action against one of its clients, who was an author, claiming payment for services it had rendered. The author countersued the law firm, claiming that the firm had unlawfully deducted amounts from its trust fund that should have been payable to him. He submitted that he was the beneficiary of the trust funds paid by a publishing firm for his book. He also claimed that his lawyer had violated the lawyer's *Code of Ethics*, having acted in a conflict of interest.

While hearing this case, I heard evidence concerning multiple conflicts that had taken place between the lawyer, the author, and a company owned by his lawyer. This included an arbitration award in a case against the company, appeals, a seizure, a bankruptcy, a sale of shares, a lawsuit against another company in which the lawyer was also involved, and a guilty plea to a fraud accusation by the lawyer's co-shareholder in the concerned company.

Generally, in a lawsuit, each party presents his case in a chronological and orderly manner. What made this case so difficult to follow was that the author had been unable to obtain an audit to determine the exact amount of money he was owed from the advance funds paid by the publisher. At trial, his counsel tried to establish the evidence through cross-examining the senior partner of the law firm. The questions were asked in a random order, and it was difficult to understand where the case was heading. What also made this case difficult was that the hearings went on for almost a year after the case had begun. Altogether there were five days of hearings that stretched over an extended period of time, with several months between each one. The evidence I heard initially was no longer fresh in my mind more than a year later.

As well, after an objection was raised by the law firm's counsel to questions relating to the firm's trust account, the hearing was suspended in order for the parties to provide written arguments. Before I had a chance to draft a decision, I went on a leave of absence due to my accident and subsequent surgery. While convalescing, I wrote an interim judgment, allowing evidence relating to the trust account. It was only several months later that I returned to work and finally heard the last part of the case.

When a trial is finished, I always review my notes, read the case law, and consider how I will resolve the lawsuit. In this case, I was stuck. Although I had concluded from examining the evidence that the senior lawyer of the law firm had violated the lawyers' *Code of Ethics*, and, as a result, he was not entitled to the legal fees the law firm sought, I had difficulty crunching the numbers of the author's claim. Ultimately, I found that the lawyer had instructed his law firm's accounting department to transfer the trust funds received from the publisher to pay his company's outstanding debts, although the money was owed to his client, the author. The senior lawyer of the law firm had offered no explanation for the fact that trust funds remitted to his law firm in connection with the author's book and which were payable to the author were used for other purposes.

The senior lawyer was clearly in a conflict of interest, placing his personal interests above those of his client, and, in doing so, he breached his obligations to the author who was his client. According to our case law, the multiple breaches of the *Code of Ethics* provided the court with discretion to reduce the legal fees sought. Based on these cases, I reduced the fees of the law firm such that the author was not obliged to pay the law firm anything. The law firm, however, was ordered to pay the author a large portion of his claim.

The judgment in this case was the last one that I wrote. It was strange that my final case turned out to be my most difficult one, but it was another case in which the underdog was seeking access to justice, and, in this instance, he obtained it.

LEGAL JARGON

While I most often wrote my judgments rather than deliver them from the bench, I noticed a recurring issue with written judgments from my colleagues. In most cases, judges do not seem to be writing for the parties in the dispute. The judgments are written in legal language, and they are dense and difficult to understand.

There are many people who read judgments: other judges, lawyers, law professors, and law students. When the decision is of public interest, journalists read them as well. However, since the judgment deals with a lawsuit between two (or more) parties, the litigants should be able to understand not only what the outcome of the case was but also how the decision was reached. But most judgments are written in language that is not comprehensible to a layperson. Archaic expressions are still used, such as null and void, will and testament, save and except, the said document, thenceforth, and so on. Many judgments continue to use Latin expressions when much simpler language could be used. Consider the words *inter alia*, *et al.*, and *a fortiori* as just a few examples. They mean "amongst others," "and others," and "all the more so," which are all more common and more readily understood.

Most judgments are written in what I call "legalese." Terms are often used that only a lawyer or another judge will understand. How many people know that a claim for damages is "prescribed" when the claim is out of time? In a judgment referring to the court's lack of information regarding the impact of the case on other proceedings before the court, the judge may state: "One thing appears clear: *Lis pendens* has not been raised here." Again, I wonder how many laypeople reading the judgment would understand that this term means a pending lawsuit (literally, a suit pending).

Not only is the language difficult to comprehend, but some judges are unable to put the testimony of each witness together to create a coherent story. Instead, they write a separate account of what each witness said in court: "The first witness stated. . . . The second witness stated. . . . The third witness stated," and so on. This makes it difficult to follow any sense of the narrative of the case. Just as unacceptable are the cases where the writing is rambling and extremely long, sometimes without any punctuation. By the time the end of a paragraph is reached, the reader must begin the paragraph again in order to recall what was stated at the outset.

Another common tendency is that of using the legal status of the parties rather than their names. Instead of referring to Mr. Smith, if he was the one who instituted the lawsuit, judges speak of the plaintiff. Similarly, rather than speaking of Mrs. Jones if she was the person who is sued, judges talk about the defendant. The issue becomes more complicated when the person who is contesting the lawsuit turns around and countersues the person who instituted the lawsuit. This lawsuit is called a cross demand, and the person who presented the cross demand becomes the defendant/cross plaintiff, while the plaintiff becomes the plaintiff/cross defendant. The language then becomes excessively difficult to read.

Consider this example:

> Cross/Defendant in its plea to the cross demand denies or ignores all the paragraphs of the cross demand and for further plea avers that there was never any agreement between the parties respecting the purchase by Cross/Plaintiff of Cross/Defendants' products.

When there is an appeal of a cross demand, the language becomes impossible to follow:

> The defendants, plaintiffs by counterclaim, appellants, claim against the third-party defendants by counterclaim respondents, in their capacity as executors of the late Geraint Patrice, a detailed report of the state of their administration of the estate, the defendants, plaintiffs by counterclaim, alleging against the latter negligence and delay.[3]

---

3 Honourable Louise Mailhot & James D Carnwath, *Decisions, Decisions . . . A Handbook for Judicial Writing* (Cowansville, QC: Éditions Yvon Blais, 1998) at 35.

I must admit that I was also guilty of the same practice. I began writing my judgments at the outset by using people's last names, but I appeared to be the only one to do so. I finally accepted using terms such as plaintiff and defendant. It made it easier to write the decision, and, at the same time, it was clear whether I was referring to the person who had instituted the lawsuit or the person who was defending against the action.

Perhaps, in discussing how judgments are written, I am overly critical of the many judgments that I have read over the years. This stems from my background: my father was a journalist and taught me how to write. He insisted that anything I wrote had to be clear, concise, and grammatically correct. As a result, I learned to write in this way. However, I am certainly not the only one who considers it important that judges learn how to write in a clear and concise manner without the use of legalese and archaic or Latin expressions.

A number of years ago, Louise Mailhot, then justice of the Court of Appeal of Quebec and James D. Carnwath, then regional senior judge in the Ontario Court of Justice, wrote a book called *Decisions, Decisions, A Handbook for Judicial Writing*. I read approvingly their criticism regarding written judgments. The following example, which comes from their book, is just one of many examples of bad writing. It illustrates how incomprehensible judgments can be when there are long sentences without punctuation:

> Although the version of events of the accused is difficult to believe taking into account the fact among other things that it would be quite astonishing for a responsible father to let his children run about in a large department store at a moment

> when the store is jammed with shoppers and even in accepting the version of the accused that does not seem to be a contradiction of the version of the witness for the crown that it was the accused himself who unpacked certain of the objects which the children had in their possession and who would have hidden them in the counters.[4]

The authors illustrate how the same text rewritten in three sentences is much clearer:

> That a responsible father would let his children run about in a crowded store is difficult to believe. Even if believed, the accused's testimony does not seem to contradict that of the witness for the Crown. She confirms having seen the father unpack certain of the goods which the children had in their possession and then hide them in the counter.[5]

If only we all learned how to write in a clear, concise manner, we would remove at least some of the difficulties that litigants face in trying to understand the outcome of their lawsuits.

---

4 *Ibid* at 21.

5 *Ibid*.

Chapter 13

The Small Claims Court

As well as the regular division of the Court of Quebec, there is also a Small Claims Division, commonly called the Small Claims Court, which, as of 2014, hears cases having a value of up to fifteen thousand dollars.

The Small Claims Court is a huge challenge for judges. Parties appear without lawyers to assist them. In fact, lawyers are not permitted to represent clients in this court and cannot even attend unless they themselves are a party to the proceedings. This has led to great difficulty since the parties, for the most part, have no idea how a trial proceeds or how to prepare for the hearing. This has also resulted in many fantastic stories about how I was addressed, how parties behaved toward each other, and how they defended themselves. In addition, it has provided a portrait of the myriad issues that bring citizens to court.

PARTIES WITHOUT LAWYERS

Because the parties in Small Claims Court are unrepresented and often do not consult a lawyer before filing their proceedings or before coming to court, they have little idea of the law that is applicable to their case. They are just as unknowledgeable about the evidence they will need to establish their claim or their defence. They do not know what is relevant, what situations require an expert witness, or what restrictions are imposed on the evidence they wish to provide. In short, the litigants do not know how to present their case.

As well, the parties often do not know how to address the judge. In one hearing, one of the parties stood up and said: "Your Majesty, I would like to show you this document." I thanked him for the promotion but assured him that Madam Justice or *Madame le juge* was sufficient as a means of addressing me. I was also called "Your Royal Highness." Again, I had to decline the title. At the other extreme, one litigant began his presentation with "Sweetie." I reminded him that I was a judge and not one of his girlfriends.

I not only received inappropriate titles but also inappropriate testimony. At the end of one of my hearings, an elderly gentleman asked me if he could add a comment. I told him that the case was over, both parties had been heard, and I would be rendering my judgment. He was insistent and said he had just one more thing to tell me. He hoped that I would allow him as it would only take a few seconds. Since we were in Small Claims Court, where we are more flexible in our rules, I gave him permission to add to his testimony. To my surprise, he said that he had been a hairdresser all his life and wanted to compliment me on my hair colour! I must admit that I was speechless as he left the courtroom.

The parties are usually very stressed when they come to Small Claims Court. Their stress is displayed in various ways, from talking too quickly to hyperventilating. In one case, I suggested that the plaintiff stand up and take a big breath to relax. When that did not work, I told her gently to repeat the exercise. She broke down in tears.

In another case involving hidden defects in a house that the buyers had purchased, the plaintiff began sobbing uncontrollably as she was relating her story. What was the problem? She had bought her dream home, but, within months of taking possession of the house, she suffered flooding that ruined the main floor of her home. After she finished her testimony, the seller began to testify. Not to be outdone by the opposing party, he also began to cry. What was the problem? He claimed he was so upset when he heard about what had happened to his beautiful home. I wondered if the parties thought that the one who cried the hardest would win their case.

One of the biggest challenges in Small Claims Court is keeping decorum in the courtroom, especially in the absence of lawyers who instruct their clients, carry out the questioning, and control the behaviour of their clients and witnesses. The parties in Small Claims Court tend to argue, scream, or hurl insults at each other. I have on many occasions told the parties they are welcome to continue their heated discussions with each other but only outside the courtroom.

The judge is far more active in the Small Claims Court than in the regular division. Since there are no lawyers involved, the judge, in addition to deciding the case after all the evidence has been heard, must determine before the hearing what legal issue is in dispute, what provision or provisions of the law apply, and what case law exists on the case in point. Once in court, the judge must explain to the parties how the case will proceed and provide some direction about the rules of evidence that must be followed. It is the judge, and not an attorney, who must question the parties and their witnesses in order to obtain the information that is necessary to be able to render a judgment. In short, the judge has a very active role to play.

The type of cases that come before the Small Claims Court cover the gamut of cases heard by the regular division of the Court of Quebec; it is essentially only the amount of money involved that differs. Although the amount that can be claimed is limited, the cases can nevertheless be complex. In addition to the usual files alleging breach of service contracts, badly done construction, hidden defects in purchased homes, unpaid professional fees, and so on, I have dealt with litigation concerning such subjects as claims relating to immigration policy and the rights of co-property owners where expert witnesses and lengthy hearings were involved. The cases I readily recall are the more unusual ones as well as the more demanding ones. I remember others because of particular circumstances or because the legal issue was unusual. Finally, there are some cases that were so typical that they all bleed together, and picking out just one is an interesting challenge. Here are some of these cases.

THE DEAD DOG

Sometimes, the cases I heard were very high stakes. Not in the monetary amount but in the emotions involved. In one case, the plaintiff sued a store after the dog she had bought from the store died suddenly. At the time of purchase, she was told to feed her dog twice a day with dry food only. She noticed that her pet was not eating very much, but she thought that was normal since it was a small dog. Because she was concerned about the amount of its intake, she began to mix canned food with the dry food to induce her pet to eat more. Sometime later, the plaintiff's neighbour, who thought the dog was very small, suggested giving the dog table food. The plaintiff considered that to be a good idea and fed her dog spaghetti. The following evening, her dog began breathing rather quickly. Shortly after, the plaintiff found her dog dead. She and her children were devastated by their loss.

She instituted an action against the store that sold her the dog, claiming that it had sold her a sick animal. In her lawsuit, she sought compensation for the cost of the dog, its cage, food, toys, vaccination costs, the autopsy, legal fees, and moral damages. A situation like hers may give rise to damages. One of my colleagues had a similar case and upheld the claim, substantiating her judgment with the provisions of the *Consumer Protection Act*.[1] However, in the case before me, contrary to that of my colleague, an autopsy had been carried out, and the plaintiff had provided the court with its findings.

According to the veterinarian's report, "there were no congenital abnormalities found in the post-mortem." The autopsy showed, as the diagnosis, that the dog had vascular decompensation due to bloat. The veterinarian noted that the dog had "died suddenly/ate a pasta meal just before." Its stomach was extremely distended with air and soft food was found in its stomach. In absence of another cause of death, he believed the death could be attributed to the bloat of the stomach.

In order to succeed in her claim, the plaintiff had to establish that the store was at fault because it was responsible for her dog's death. However, the dog had received vaccinations when it was a few months old, and there was no indication at that time that the veterinarian found the dog abnormally small for its age. Moreover, no congenital condition had been found. In short, the evidence did not

---

Chapter 13

1 *Consumer Protection Act*, CQLR c P-40.1.

substantiate the plaintiff's claim that she had been sold an unhealthy dog. The store could not be blamed for the bloat suffered by the dog, which appeared to be caused by the food that it was fed and which was the likely cause of death.

The plaintiff and her children were very attached to their pet and were inconsolable when it died. I had a great deal of sympathy for them and said so in my judgment. However, I was unable to grant them the recourse they sought. What I did not say in my judgment was that it appeared that the plaintiff herself was responsible for the death of her dog.

THE FABRICATION OF KIPPAS

In another case, a Jewish family had ordered yarmulkes (skullcaps or *kippas*) from a manufacturer for the bar mitzva[2] of their son. The kippas, which were custom made, were inscribed on the inside with the son's name and the date of the event. Before they were made, the company showed the family an example of the product, and the family agreed to the production. Just prior to the bar mitzva, the family made a second order and signed another contract with respect to this order. When the kippas were made, the family would not accept the finished product, claiming they were badly sewn and were not presentable. They refused to pay for them. The manufacturer sued the family. Obviously, with the name and date inscribed inside the kippas, they could not be resold to anyone else.

At the hearing, I heard the evidence and asked for an example of one of the kippas that the family had refused to

---

2 A bar mitzva is a religious ceremony held in the Jewish religion when a boy turns thirteen years of age. In the case of a girl, the ceremony is called a bat mitzva.

accept. The company could not provide the original kippa that the family had seen and agreed to purchase, but they told me that it was identical in nature to those that had been delivered as final products. I was provided with several to examine.

In law, "every person has a duty to honour his contractual undertakings." When the person fails to respect those obligations, he is responsible to pay for the damages that the other party has incurred. Clearly, the family had contracted to buy a certain number of kippas, and the defendant had respected its obligation to manufacture them. The question remained as to the quality. Was it so unacceptable, as the family claimed, that they should not be required to pay for them?

I consider myself to have very high standards, but I could find no evidence of the poor sewing or appearance the family had claimed. Had the original kippa been of much better quality? I found it hard to believe that was the case. I wished I could see the original product. Since I could not, I had to make my decision based purely on the quality of what was in front of me. Looking over the kippas, I could see nothing at all wrong with the way they were made. Accordingly, I held the family responsible to pay the defendant in accordance with the contract they had signed.

After rendering my judgment, I went home and looked at a package on top of my cupboard. In it, I kept a bag of kippas I had received from various bar mitzvas and weddings that I had attended over the years. Judges can only base their decisions on the evidence that is presented in court. But I was nevertheless curious about the quality of the kippas I had collected. Their quality varied somewhat. I had one that was made of suede, and it was by far the most luxurious. However, all the others looked no different from the ones the family had refused to accept. Although I had already decided there was nothing wrong with the kippas that had been produced for the family in question, and could not change the judgment I had rendered, I nevertheless felt better about my decision after I had examined my personal collection.

THE MOTORCYCLE REPAIR

While judges can question the parties and witnesses in the Small Claims Court and make comments about a case, they keep personal information to themselves. Unintentionally, in one case, I broke this unwritten rule.

We dealt regularly with car repairs in Small Claims Court. Lawsuits involving motorcycle repairs were not quite as common, but we nevertheless heard such cases from time to time. In a memorable case, the plaintiff had left his Yamaha motorcycle for repair at a shop that indicated that it specialized in these repairs. At the beginning of the hearing, the plaintiff described his motorcycle. It was a Yamaha four-cylinder racing bike. It was the same bike that my husband rode. I have no idea why I blurted out: "I know that motorcycle; we have one in our garage." As soon as the words were out of my mouth, I wanted to capture them and erase them. First, there was no reason to reveal personal information in a hearing, and it was a most improper statement to make. Second, the motorcycle in our garage was not my bike, but my husband's. Most importantly, I knew nothing about his motorcycle or that of the plaintiff's other than the fact that my husband's bike was a Yamaha and that it was blue.

The plaintiff looked elated. He felt that he no longer had to worry about an older blonde woman (namely me) deciding what his bike needed with respect to repairs or whether the repairs were badly done by the defendant, as he contended. The plaintiff believed that he had hit the jackpot—a judge who not only understood how motorcycles worked but also a judge who even rode the same bike as he did. I could not at that point say that I had misspoken. I listened to the evidence and took copious notes. I nodded when I considered it appropriate to do so and tried my best to follow the evidence regarding the minute details of the pieces of the engine and the repairs that had been done.

Initially, I was hoping to put it all down on paper and then turn to my husband to bail me out. However, I realized by the end of the hearing that the garage owner had not provided any estimate of the repairs before carrying them out, contrary to the *Consumer Protection Act*. Ultimately, I was saved from having to evaluate each and every one of the repairs and determine their validity. I could base my judgment on the failure of the garage to follow the requisite procedures established by law and render my judgment in favour of the plaintiff accordingly. However, I did learn an important lesson: no more impromptu comments in the courtroom.

THE BANK THEFT

While we regularly heard cases involving hidden defects, shoddy construction work, and broken service contracts, cases dealing with bank theft were highly unusual. One such case sticks in my mind because it felt like something that could happen to anyone.

In this case, Mr. P. went to his bank to pay some bills. When he entered the bank's outer vestibule, he noticed a vagrant person crouched in the premises. Mr. P. paid his bill using the bank machine and then went across the street to buy some goods. He arrived at the cash register and realized that he did not have his bank card with him. He immediately returned to the bank, but his card was no longer in the machine. The vagrant person was not in the lobby either. Mr. P. reported the loss to the bank and was told that fifteen hundred dollars had been removed from his accounts. He made a claim with the bank, but it denied any responsibility. Mr. P. then sued the bank.

The photographs presented in evidence showed that Mr. P. had left the bank before he terminated his session and that his bank card was still in the banking machine. Since the session had not been closed and the process was active, the next person to arrive could make further withdrawals without having to provide Mr. P.'s pin number. The contract between the bank and its clients states:

> No one but you is permitted to use your pin. If someone obtains your client card and your pin in a way that enables them to be used together, you may be liable for their use of your client card. ... You are responsible to take reasonable precautions to keep your client card and pin safe. ... Always make sure that you can see your client card at all times when you are using it for a POS transaction. ... Always remember to take your client card and transaction record after a transaction is completed. ... It is our responsibility to show on a balance of probability that you have contributed to someone else's unauthorized use of your client card and pin.

Mr. P. claimed that he was not liable since he did not intentionally allow a third party to use his client card and that the bank had to show that he contributed to the unauthorized use by another person. I consulted our legal services to see if there was any case law on the subject, but they could find nothing. What was interesting was that the lawyers in our legal department were evenly divided as to the outcome of the case. Half of them believed that the bank was responsible, while the remainder considered that Mr. P. was responsible for his own loss.

After a great deal of thought, I concluded that I could not order the bank to compensate Mr. P. I took into consideration the agreement between the bank and its clients where it states that clients are responsible for taking reasonable precautions to keep their client cards and pins safe and must assure that they can see their client cards at all times when using one for a transaction. In this case, after paying his bill, Mr. P. did not ensure that he had his client card with him; he left the premises without removing his card from the banking machine and without finishing his transaction. By leaving the bank with his transaction process still active, his client card could be—and was—easily used by another person.

In short, even though Mr. P. did not intend to allow anyone else to withdraw funds from his account, I considered that he contributed to the unauthorized use of his card by another person and, in fact, that he facilitated the theft by his actions. He was negligent in his handling of his client card, and his negligence constituted a fault, irrespective of whether it was intended or not, and so I dismissed his case. However, because of the particular circumstances of the case, I did not impose any court costs on Mr. P.

TRAVEL CASES

Lawsuits against travel agents and tour operators are common. The many cases I heard dealt with ruined holidays because of misrepresentations regarding hotel accommodations, inadequate services that were provided, airlines that failed to respect bookings or overbooked, and various other aspects of a planned vacation that went wrong. One case stands out because it was one of the worst lawsuits concerning a "ruined holiday."

In this case, several plaintiffs sued their agent and tour operator because of the unacceptable accommodations they were given during an all-inclusive one-week trip to Cuba. Upon arrival at their destination, they were told that the upscale hotel they had selected was overbooked. They were given the choice of another hotel several hours away, which was not on the beach, or a two-star hotel a few minutes away from their chosen hotel. They chose the hotel closer to the one they had initially chosen. Their stay turned out to be disastrous.

The photographs that the plaintiffs presented in court showed a bug-infested hotel room, unfit to stay in. The sheets on their beds were stained, the faucet was rusted, the phones were defective, and there were cockroaches in the bathroom. There was no access to the beach, and the bus that was to bring them to another hotel for breakfast was an hour late, such that there was no meal available when they arrived. In addition, because of the bus schedule, they missed the end of the evening shows and the discotheque at the other hotel.

After complaining about their accommodations, they were transferred to a bungalow outside of the upscale hotel.

These accommodations were also unacceptable. The windows were covered with a sheet, the bathroom floor was cracked, and there was no hot water and no lock on the door. The tour operator claimed that, when it discovered there was no space at the hotel the plaintiffs had chosen, it offered them another hotel of a superior category on a beach—a fact that the plaintiffs denied.

After hearing the evidence of both parties, I sided with the plaintiffs' version. It was not conceivable that they would choose a lower-ranked hotel without access to the beach had they been told they could have stayed at a superior hotel on the beach. The travel agent and tour operator had advertised an upscale hotel situated directly on the beach with three meals provided as well as various activities, including shows and a discotheque in the evenings. The evidence showed that the plaintiffs were unable to fully enjoy the vacation they had booked. They were not provided with the facilities or services indicated in the brochure. Instead, there was no access to the beach and, virtually, no services available.

According to Quebec law, agents and wholesalers or operators in the field of travel have what we call the "obligation of result"—that is, they are responsible for providing products that correspond with descriptions they give whether the descriptions are provided verbally, in writing, in illustrations, or in their publicity. In this case, since the travel agent and the tour operator failed to provide the lodgings and the service that they had advertised in their brochure, I concluded that they were liable for the prejudice suffered by the plaintiffs and awarded the plaintiffs compensation equal to the cost of their trip.

BOTCHED RENOVATIONS

Other typical cases in the Small Claims Court concerned renovations that were poorly carried out. Sometimes, the contractor or service provider sued to obtain the payment the parties had agreed upon for the work to be done. In other cases, the client who paid the contractor or service provider sued to recuperate money that had already been paid for work that the client claimed was badly done. In either case, the issue revolved around whether the contractor's work was satisfactory since a contractor, or a service provider, must act in accordance with "the rules of art."

Any one of the cases I heard could serve as an example. In each case, I not only heard testimony, but I also saw photographs of the work that had allegedly been poorly carried out. As the expression goes, "a picture is worth a thousand words."

In one case where a client sued a contractor complaining that he paid for renovations that were shoddy and incomplete, the evidence was clear, but the contract made with the contractor proved to be problematic for the client. The plaintiff easily established that the work was not only unfinished but also incredibly sloppy. It included streaky paint, unpainted edges, and an unpainted doorframe and cabinet interiors. There was paint covering light switch plates, and one wall was painted without first removing a mirror. The ventilation was improperly installed and not sealed, such that the condensed air went into the stairwell and the paint in that area had peeled. The kitchen cabinets needed to be cut but were not done, and the premises were left uncleaned. The plaintiff had clearly established that the work was unacceptable.

However, the contract was verbal. There was no written evidence as to the cost of the services provided. The client showed that he had withdrawn various amounts of cash from his bank account on different dates. However, cash withdrawals, without an indication as to whom the money was paid, do not constitute proof of payment. Fortunately for the client, the contractor admitted to having received a certain amount of money for the paint job. That was the only sum that I was able to grant him. This case is a good example of the many cases I heard about poor workmanship. It also shows the problem that a party faces when a contract is verbal. There is nothing to establish the terms of the contract or the amounts of money the parties have agreed upon for the work. In addition, since the payment is often in cash, without any receipt, the party who is suing has difficulty proving what he has actually paid.

The plaintiff has the burden of proof; unless he can establish his claim to the satisfaction of the court, he will not succeed in obtaining the monetary compensation he seeks. In this case, the client only obtained partial compensation since he had neither a written contract nor any proof of the amount he had paid.

In other cases, the problem was a failure on the part of the client to send a demand letter to the contractor requiring the contractor to return and redo the inadequate work or finish the job. The demand letter is essential. It provides the contractor with the opportunity to rectify his work. Unless the situation is urgent, the claim is virtually always dismissed when such a letter is not sent.

INSURANCE CLAIMS

Insurance lawsuits were common. The insured, having suffered damage, presents a claim with his insurance provider; when the claim is refused, the insured institutes a lawsuit.

Typically, the reasons for refusal by an insurance company are that the insured has lied or exaggerated the loss, has failed to pay the premiums on a regular basis, has omitted important information in his declaration, or has made a false declaration when the policy was taken out. When I received an insurance claim, I noted that one company, in particular, was frequently the defendant in my courtroom. I had no explanation for why some insurance companies were sued more than others, except perhaps the tendency by one particular company to refuse as many claims as it could.

One case involved a theft of property in a car owned by a security guard. The insured immediately contacted his insurance company and reported the loss of a number of items, including a laptop, a bulletproof vest and part of his uniform, earphones, and other goods. The plaintiff met with the claims adjuster and underwent an investigation. He was further interrogated by the insurance company's attorney and was accused of lying and committing fraud. The insurance company refused the claim, maintaining that the loss of the laptop, which had been reported after the initial declaration of loss, was not credible or probable. The insured then filed a lawsuit.

Many of the problems the insured encountered in the file stemmed from the misunderstandings of the police agent who took the report. She was francophone and claimed that contradictory statements were made when, in fact, she simply did not fully understand what the insured had said to her in English. One such example was the insured's statement that the computer was a gift and that it had been purchased in the United States. The agent understood that the insured had purchased the computer in the United States and, accordingly, that it could not have been a gift. The insured was unable to provide proof of the purchase since the computer had been a present given to him, but he was able to show photographs of his wife and child in front of the laptop, which demonstrated the existence of the laptop and the model.

Other problems stemmed from the fact that the laptop was reported missing two days after the theft and after the initial declaration of loss. It was only then that the insured realized that it was, in fact, missing and had been in his car after bringing it to a meeting with friends. Such a situation is not unusual. Moreover, the testimony of several of his friends established that he had brought his laptop to a meeting on the evening of the theft.

The insurance company placed a great deal of importance on the fact that the insured could not describe the computer's technical properties. The insured explained that he was not "a tech guy." He could describe its colour and the location of the mouse but not how much RAM it had or the size of its hard drive. I did not consider such lack of knowledge about a computer's technological aspects as abnormal; most people would be unable to answer any similar questions about their own computer's properties.

Credibility is key in determining whether an insured is telling the truth or not. In this case, the evidence convinced me that the insured did own a laptop and that it had been stolen. Another fact in his favour was that, as a security guard, he regularly handled millions of dollars in cash; he was vetted for the position and had passed a lie detector test. It seemed to me that there was little likelihood of the insured making a false claim that could potentially impact his job. I granted him the compensation he was seeking for his loss but rejected his claim for damages for trouble and inconvenience, alleged harassment, and abuse from the insurance company. The insurance company carried out an investigation, which it was entitled to do.

THE WEDDING VIDEOGRAPHER

Having a record of a wedding is precious for any couple. Due to the emotions involved, it is easy for me to remember a case where the videographer failed to take a video at a wedding. A photography studio that provided wedding services, including photography and videography, subcontracted some work to a photographer, who would be the studio's exclusive photographer for several weddings that summer. During the execution of the first wedding contract, the studio's videographer asked the photographer where the next location would be. The photographer advised him as to the site of the outdoor photographs and suggested he follow when the photographer left. The videographer instead left on his own without waiting for the photographer and without providing the photographer with his telephone number.

The photographer headed for the location of the photo shoot, but all the surrounding streets were blocked by a parade, and the photographs had to be taken at another place. The photographer attempted, without success, to reach the wedding planner in order to contact the videographer. Since the videographer had left before the parade started, and was unaware of the change in venue, he managed to arrive at the original location intended for the photo shoot, but the wedding party was not there, and, consequently, no videography footage was taken.

The newly married couple obviously complained to the studio. Rather than blaming the videographer, the studio blamed the photographer for sending the videographer to the wrong location. They cancelled the photographer's remaining contracts for the summer. Given that weddings are booked well in advance, the photographer was unable to book new events on the dates that the photography studio had cancelled. The photographer sued the studio for the loss of his remaining contracts.

The studio claimed that the photographer had changed the location without informing the videographer of the change. That was true. However, the videographer had been instructed to follow the photographer, and he had failed to do so. He left on his own, without providing the photographer with any means of contacting him. The photographer was not responsible for the change in venue. He was prevented from reaching the planned location because of the parade. He was also not responsible for not contacting the videographer since he did not have the videographer's phone number. He even tried to reach him through the wedding planner and was unable to do so.

The studio cancelled several of the photographer's contracts, which our law allows it to do. However, although a client can put an end to a contract, he must pay the service provider for the work performed before the notice of cancellation and for any prejudice suffered as a result of the cancellation.

In this case, I concluded that the photographer was entitled to be paid for the work he had done before the contracts were cancelled. He was also entitled to damages since it was impossible for him to replace the contracts that had been cancelled on such short notice. The amounts awarded were discretionary, as is always the case for damages in such lawsuits. As for the couple who were married, they received a reduction in the price from the studio since no videography was taken of them at the intended location. On the other hand, I presume that the reduction in price did not compensate for the fact that they had no video footage of one of the most important days of their lives.

Chapter 14

Judging Judges

While judges decide the cases assigned to them, they may also find themselves judged. Judges are subjected to discipline when their behaviour falls outside the strict rules of their *Judicial Code of Ethics*.[1] Their conduct must be without reproach, both inside and outside the courtroom. This chapter looks at how judges are expected to act, whether they can "be bought," and what consequences can be applied if they fail to respect their obligations. I provide some examples of the errors that judges can make in judging, and what we do to mitigate those possible errors.

CAN A JUDGE BE BRIBED?

At one of the first conferences that I attended as a judge, the topic was whether judges can be bribed. In the 1990s, a journalist had documented and produced a film detailing how the public viewed our judicial system. The persons who were interviewed were asked whether they thought judges could be bribed. The majority thought it was, in fact, possible. I was rather taken aback by the low esteem the general population had for the justice system. I would

Chapter 14

1 *Judicial Code of Ethics*, CQLR c T-16, r 1.

hope that, with information being more readily available to the public through the internet, and the attempts by various non-profit organizations to render justice more accessible, the image of our courts has changed since the time that documentary was made.

Judges are expected to act in such a way that their conduct is beyond reproach. Their conduct both in and out of court is subject to public scrutiny, to the scrutiny of the Council of the Quebec Judiciary, and to public comment. In the case of federally appointed judges, one of the first principles enunciated in the booklet entitled *Ethical Principles for Judges* is that "judges must exercise their judicial functions independently and free of extraneous influence"; they must firmly reject any attempt outside the proper process to influence their decisions in any matter that is before the court.[2]

Perhaps, in the distant past, judges were not very well paid and, thus, were more likely to be influenced by money and willing to accept a bribe. That is certainly not the case today. Not only is the revenue of judges considerable, but the pension a judge receives is also extremely generous. The risk of losing a prestigious position, a generous salary, and substantial revenue at retirement is simply not worth any amount of money that could be offered to a judge as a bribe in an attempt to have him render a decision in a particular way.

Throughout my entire career, there was only one occasion where an attempt was made to improperly affect my decision. Another judge advised me that a friend was the defendant in a case that I was hearing. I wondered whether

2 Canadian Judicial Council, *Ethical Principles for Judges*, Catalogue No JU11-4/2004E (Ottawa: Canadian Judicial Council, 1998), ch 2, s 2.

that colleague had brought this fact to my attention in order to ensure that I would not rule against the friend. I was most displeased by the information, and I ignored it while hearing the case. As it turned out, the evidence was such that I did not find the defendant responsible for the claim made against him. However, if I had found him responsible for having violated the provisions of the law that applied in his case, I would have rendered the judgment against him, in the same way as I would have rendered my decision against any other person in a similar situation. I nevertheless considered that the comment made by that colleague was an attempt to influence me and was totally improper.

Judicial independence is assured to guarantee the impartiality of a judge. This protects a judge from any form of pressure, whether it comes from the government, pressure groups, the public, or the media. Citizens who appear before a judge must have the certainty that they will be judged by an impartial judge. They must also have the certainty that the judgment rendered will be based solely on the evidence presented in court and the law in effect at that time.[3]

As the Honourable François Rolland, retired chief justice of the Montreal Superior Court, explained in an article published in *Le Devoir*, the independence of a judge is assured in a number of ways: a judge cannot be removed so long as his behaviour is appropriate; he is provided with financial security by receiving a sufficient revenue that removes him from any influence, and he has institutional independence—that is, his assignments are given to him by the judges in authority and not by political figures.[4]

---

3 François Rolland, "Libre opinion: l'indépendance judiciaire et l'intégrité des juges," *Le Devoir* (21 September 2011).

4 *Ibid.*

I have no hesitation in stating that any attempt at influencing a judge, whether it be by a superior, a colleague, a lawyer, a litigant, or any other person, would be immediately rebuffed by any judge I worked with or knew.

JUDICIAL RESTRAINT

Judges are governed by a set of rules or ethical principles that include the requirement to respect what we refer to as the "obligation of reserve." The *Judicial Code of Ethics* for judges in Quebec states that, in his public behaviour, the judge must show reserve, courtesy, and serenity.[5] The conduct of judges must be above reproach in the view of reasonable, fair-minded, and informed persons. This is to ensure public confidence in the judiciary and respect for the institution, which is essential to an effective judicial system. The courts cannot carry out their mission if they do not have the confidence of the public. In order to maintain respect and confidence in the judiciary, judges must keep themselves removed from any controversy that can affect their appearance of impartiality. Judges must also strive to ensure that their conduct, both in and out of court, maintains confidence in their impartiality and that of the judiciary.

This means that even a judge's behaviour after hours is subject to scrutiny. On one occasion, during a court-organized party, one of the judges allegedly had a little too much to drink. When the judge went to get her car in the underground parking lot in the courthouse, and drove to the exit, she considered that the staff took too long to open the door and allow her to drive out. She ranted

---

5 *Judicial Code of Ethics*, above note 1, s 8.

and raved and called the staff all kinds of inappropriate names, including "*imbecile*," "*bande d'épais*" (thick heads), and "*bande d'incompétent*" (group of incompetents), incapable of opening a door.

Her actions were recorded, and a complaint was made to the Council of the Quebec Judiciary. Her behaviour was deemed to be most inappropriate. The investigation committee pointed to two provisions of the *Judicial Code of Ethics* that state that judges must fulfill their role with integrity, dignity, and honour and that, as previously indicated, judges must show reserve, courtesy, and serenity in their public behaviour.[6] The investigation committee recommended that the council reprimand the judge in question given her troublesome and deplorable behaviour.

Because of the various ethical principles that guide judges, the ability of judges to express themselves in public is limited. This limitation flows from the obligation to respect the independence, impartiality, dignity, honour, authority, and legitimacy of the judiciary. As a result, judges at the Court of Quebec cannot participate in public debates. The federal *Judges Act* specifically indicates that judges have an ethical obligation to avoid involvement in public debate that may unnecessarily expose them to political attack or be inconsistent with the dignity of judicial office.[7] Judges cannot publicly express their opinions on political issues, on the government's position on various issues, or on current events.[8] Judges cannot be outspoken on any subject that can be construed to be controversial.

6 *Ibid*, ss 2, 8.

7 This Act governs the behaviour of judges appointed to the Federal Court and to the Superior Court in Quebec, which is known as the Supreme Court in the provinces outside Quebec.

8 Canadian Judicial Council, above note 2, ch 6, s D-3.

They are restricted from expressing their criticism and from any discussions that could compromise the confidence and respect of the function.

In addition, judges cannot defend themselves when they are subjected to criticism. When we refer to the obligation of reserve, this is not only to maintain impartiality but also judges' appearance of impartiality. When a judgment is criticized, whether by an individual or by the media, the judge cannot explain or justify it. It is up to the Court of Appeal to confirm or overturn a judgment. Judges must also be serene when they hear cases and must have the respect and confidence of the public for our judicial system to function properly. It is up to all the intervenors in the justice system to take great care to ensure that this respect and confidence is not jeopardized.

I do not recall receiving any formal training on this subject, although I was aware of the *Judicial Code of Ethics*. Even if the obligation of reserve was not specifically spelled out, I understood when I became a judge that my opinions in public were necessarily limited. When political or controversial issues were raised, despite having been very outspoken on many of these subjects before I was named a judge, I remained silent, except if I was with very close friends. Even then, I was careful about what I said.

The only places where I did not feel constrained were in my own home with my husband and in my office with my assistant Josette. I could say whatever I wished about any subject, even if it was critical of a political position, a government action, a broadcast, or a controversial issue. I had full confidence in both my husband and Josette; I was certain that neither would reveal my personal opinions.

As a judge, I never felt that it was a great imposition to refrain from speaking openly or to keep my thoughts to myself. However, since my retirement, I do enjoy being able to express myself freely. I have been reproached at times about some of my views, and I accept the criticism. On the other hand, the freedom to say what I think about any particular issue is nevertheless somewhat liberating.

DISCIPLINING JUDGES

When my colleague's behaviour was called into question, I mentioned that she was investigated by the Conseil de la Magistrature (Council of the Quebec Judiciary). This body is composed of judges, lawyers, and members from the general public and is responsible for overseeing the conduct of judges appointed by the Quebec government. It is concerned with reprehensible conduct or a breach of ethics; its role is not to evaluate a decision that a litigant considers to be unsatisfactory or wrong (such cases are handled by the Court of Appeal).

When a complaint is made, the council first evaluates the allegation. If the council concludes that it does not warrant any further investigation, the complaint is dismissed. If the council decides, after an investigation, that an inquiry is warranted, it carries out this procedure. Following the inquiry, the council can reject the complaint, or it can impose a reprimand if it decides that discipline is justified. In extreme cases, it can make a recommendation to the minister of justice that the judge in question be removed from office.

The typical complaints that are filed against judges allege that the judge was impolite, impatient, aggressive, condescending, partial, or prevented a party from expressing himself or presenting evidence. In such cases, the Council of the Quebec Judiciary will listen to the recording of the trial to determine whether the allegation raised is valid or not. More often than not, the litigant is not happy with the judgment that was rendered, and the complaint is simply a disguised appeal. However, dissatisfaction with the outcome of a case is not a valid basis for a grievance, nor is it, in itself, a reason for the council to conduct an inquiry.

In a case where one of my colleagues had a hearing before the *comité d'enquête* (the investigation committee of the council), the complainant alleged that the judge displayed aggressive behaviour, made inappropriate comments, and showed a lack of courtesy through a critical tone of voice. The judge in question claimed that he was not feeling well that day but believed that it was important to handle his assignments and show up in court. The Council of the Quebec Judiciary did not agree and considered that the judge should have stayed home if he was sick. It found that the judge's language and comments violated his obligation of dignity, honour, impartiality, courtesy, and serenity. While his behaviour was considered inappropriate, the council did not believe it warranted his dismissal. It concluded that a reprimand was the appropriate sanction.

In a more serious case, the investigation committee held a hearing following a grievance about a judge who had invoked deficiencies in the evidence of one of the parties and insisted that the parties attempt to settle their case, refusing to hear them. This was not the first time that this particular judge had been brought to a hearing on a complaint of the same nature. The committee concluded that the judge did not understand his judicial and ethical obligations—namely, to hear the parties and render a judgment. Since he refused to exercise the function for which he had been named, only one conclusion was appropriate: that of his removal from office. The committee accordingly recommended that the minister of justice remove that judge from office.

The Canadian Judicial Council carries out the same role as the Council of the Quebec Judiciary with respect to complaints filed against judges who sit on the Superior Court or the Court of Appeal. Like many judges at the Court of Quebec, particularly in cases involving the Small Claims Court, I had a few dealings with the Council of the Quebec Judiciary. While I never had a case heard by the investigation committee, it was nevertheless upsetting when a claim was made against me. The following are accounts of two cases that came before the council.

THE PALESTINIAN-CANADIAN COMPLAINT

I had been on the bench for less than two years when I was advised that a complaint had been submitted against me. I was shocked and understandably upset. I was also embarrassed, and because of my embarrassment, I did not speak to any of my colleagues about my misfortune. After closing the door to our office, which I usually left open, my assistant Josette and I listened to the recording of the hearing. I reread my judgment and then sat down and wrote a detailed account of the evidence presented at trial, the research I had done, and the consultation I had carried out before I wrote my judgment.

The case concerned a Canadian of Palestinian descent who was suing his travel agent. The travel agent had booked the man on a flight to the West Bank via the Tel Aviv airport. After the tickets were purchased, the complainant was told by a third party that Palestinians born in the West Bank were precluded from using the Tel Aviv airport. He cancelled the trip, claiming that the cancellation was involuntary, but the travel agent would not return his money. When the man objected, the travel agent told him that the tickets were not refundable and that he had no knowledge of Israel's landing policy.

I first had to determine whether the complainant would actually have been unable to land in Tel Aviv. He had provided no evidence to substantiate his claim. His contention that Israel had a landing policy that meant he would not have been able to land at the Tel Aviv airport came from a third, unnamed party and was, therefore, hearsay. In addition, I considered whether a travel agent (who has an obligation to act in the best interests of his client) had an obligation to give information regarding warnings issued by foreign governments. While travel agents should know what limitations apply to Canadian citizens travelling abroad, the alleged problem in this case related to the status of the complainant and the members of his family in relation to another country's policies, not as a Canadian but, rather, as another national.

I concluded that it was not reasonable to require that a travel agent verify the religious and/or ethnic background of every customer with respect to travel everywhere in the world in order to provide appropriate advice regarding the impact of a foreign country's policies on a particular client. I stated in my judgment that the travel agent's failure to advise the complainant of any restrictions set by Israel in its landing policy, if such restrictions existed, did not constitute a fault for which the travel agent was liable.

Before rendering my judgment, I took additional steps to verify and obtain information about Israel's travel policy. When the complainant was unable to provide any evidence to support his claim that he could not land in Tel Aviv, I rescheduled the hearing to give him another chance to obtain the proof that he needed; at this second hearing, he failed to provide any new information. I also asked the court's representatives to contact the Israeli consulate regarding the alleged policy. However, the consulate invoked its diplomatic immunity and declined to send a representative to the next hearing. I then consulted the court's legal services to obtain information about the government's travel advisories as well as a legal opinion regarding the position I wished to adopt. The legal opinion provided to me by the court's legal services confirmed the position of the travel agent and not that of the complainant.

I went to all this trouble because I wanted to ensure that my judgment would be sound and without bias. Given the fact that I am Jewish and the complainant in this case was of Palestinian background, I did not want to be accused of any partiality. But, despite all the care I had taken to render a judgment that was legally correct, the plaintiff had filed a complaint against me. He was displeased with my analysis and my conclusions.

The Council of the Quebec Judiciary advised me that the plaintiff's allegations had been rejected. It was, like many such complaints, a disguised appeal of my decision. I was very relieved.

After I received the decision of the council, I broached the subject with one of my colleagues, telling him what had transpired. He laughed and jokingly said: "You're not a real judge until a complaint has been filed against you." I learned that many other judges had received complaints from litigants. This most often occurred in cases in the Small Claims Court, where the parties are not represented by lawyers and therefore do not have the necessary legal advice to understand what constitutes a valid grievance against a judge.

DAMAGE TO PROPERTY

During the rest of my time on the bench, only one other complaint was filed against me. This case concerned a woman who was sued for allegedly having deliberately damaged the plaintiff's property. I concluded from the evidence that the plaintiff had established her case, and I condemned the defendant to pay for the plaintiff's damages.

The defendant filed a complaint and contended that I did not understand the evidence. I read her submission, remembered the case, and did not even bother to respond to the Council of the Quebec Judiciary. I knew that I had not breached any rules of behaviour—once again, her complaint was simply an attempt to appeal my judgment. Her case, like the previous one, was summarily dismissed by the council without being brought to an investigation. There were no further complaints about my judgments for the remainder of my career.

DO JUDGES ERR?

While many complaints against judges are appeals in disguise, there are certainly cases where a judge has failed to understand the evidence or where an error in fact or in law has been made. The correct recourse for such an error is not a complaint against the judge but, rather, an appeal of the judgment. However, not every erroneous judgment is appealed. When I refer to an erroneous judgment, I am not considering cases where a colleague may come to a different conclusion than I would. That can and does happen, and neither decision is necessarily in error. What I am referring to here are cases where a decision is actually wrong in law.

In writing about this subject, I tried to recall whether I had rendered any such judgments. It is difficult to know whether I might have committed a mistake since, once a judgment was written, I immediately turned my mind to the next case that had to be decided. Unless a judgment I wrote was appealed, there was little reason for me to consider it or determine whether it was wrong.

However, I do recall two particular cases where I erred. In one instance, a contractor had rebuilt the balcony of a client, and the client later sued him for allegedly shoddy work, including an uneven balcony. At the hearing, the contractor explained that the client had given him specific instructions regarding the level of a step leading from the door to the balcony. He contended it was the specifications of the client that was the cause of the lack of evenness in the balcony. I ruled in favour of the contractor and dismissed the client's case.

It was one of my first cases at the Court of Quebec when I was still in my learning curve. I talked about the case to one of my colleagues after the decision had already been written and issued. She explained that contractors are required to act in the best interests of their clients in a prudent and diligent way. Moreover, they must respect "usual practice and the rules of art," which includes regulations, building codes, and proper construction methods. They cannot follow a client's instructions if the instructions do not conform to these principles and rules. My judgment was therefore incorrect. The contractor had carried out the work according to the instructions he had received from his client, which were contrary to the building code rather than in line with the rules of the trade, which is required by law. Following that discussion, I determined and applied the rules of the art or the trade in all my subsequent cases.

The other case involved an application for a restricted driver's licence. A doctor whose licence had been revoked because he earned too many demerit points claimed that he worked on the other side of the city and was often on call; he needed the use of his car to reach the hospital quickly in such circumstances. At the time, I considered the reason he provided to have merit, and I granted the application.

I subsequently read a judgment of the Superior Court in which the judge had overturned a decision of one of my colleagues who, in very similar circumstances, had granted a restricted licence. According to the Superior Court, and as you may remember from an earlier chapter, a restricted licence is granted solely to carry out a person's employment, such as that of a delivery person, a taxi driver, or someone whose job is on the road. It is not to allow the applicant to use a vehicle to reach his job. In my case, since the doctor's position was carried out in a hospital, he was not entitled by law to have a restricted permit. My judgment, as I learned afterward, was erroneous. It was some comfort to me, however, that I was not the only judge who had erred in granting a restricted permit in such a case.

Chapter 15

Sexism, Discrimination, and Change

When I was a young woman, I naively assumed that sexism and discrimination did not exist in the field of law. I thought that people who spent their life pursuing justice would be better at upholding it. Unfortunately, the legal profession is no different from any other profession or trade.

While I experienced a large amount of sexism during my tenure in the law, particularly as a lawyer, I have been pleased to witness a significant change in the field over the years. There has been a large increase in the number of women in law, and, as a result, there is less sexism than there was decades ago when I began my career. On the other hand, our courts still do not adequately reflect the population that they serve. More diversity is still necessary in all branches of our judicial system.

A JEWISH JUDGE IN QUEBEC

While I was still in law school, I began applying for a job as an articling student, mainly in large firms. Having excellent marks enabled me to easily obtain interviews. What I remember most about this process were some of the questions that I was asked, many of which I found offensive. At one well-known prestigious firm, a senior partner, who interviewed me in his spacious corner office, asked me how I felt about working at a Christian law firm. I was startled by his question. "I thought I was applying to a law firm, not to a religious organization," I said. "Well, I'm familiar with your Uncle Harold. Since he's Jewish, I know you must be . . . of the same persuasion." I was furious. "Yes," I said. "I am Jewish, but I can't imagine what that has to do with my application."

Although I was angry about the questioning, I had to maintain my calm. To my surprise, this law firm was one of the ones that ultimately offered me a position as an articling student. In another firm, I was questioned about my religious practices. Somewhat on edge, I asked them why I was being asked whether I was observant. The partners explained that they wanted to determine whether I could work on Friday evenings and on Saturdays if it was required. At least the question was pertinent to the practice of law at that firm and not a disguised racist question. Other questions dealt with my marital status and whether I intended to become pregnant in the near future. It was a time when there were not many women working as lawyers, and most law firms did not have a clear maternity policy. Questions of this nature posed no problem—I was not married then, and I had no intention of having children as a single mother—but they were still frustrating to field.

During the course of my career, I experienced much sexism but only one instance of racism. I have a vivid recollection of this plenary session, presided over by a journalist, at one of our annual conferences. I must admit that I do not remember the topic of discussion, but I do recall one of the judges, who I did not know, raise the issue about the composition of the Supreme Court of Canada.

He stated that there were too many Jewish judges on the Supreme Court. I was shocked by his comment. Had I had more time to think, I would have said that I thought the justices on the Supreme Court of Canada were appointed for their competence and not for their religion. But I did not respond as I wished I had.

I nevertheless did speak up. I asked whether anyone could tell the journalist how many Jewish judges there were on the Court of Quebec. No one replied, and I sat down. The journalist then turned to the chief justice and asked him if he knew the answer to the question I had posed. The chief justice said: "There is one Jewish judge—and she just sat down." Although this was the only such case of racism during the time I was on the bench, it obviously affected me. After all these years, I recall every word that was said in that room.

WOMEN IN LAW

If a woman today says she is a lawyer, few eyebrows are raised. However, the entry of a large number of women in what was a traditionally male profession is still relatively new. When I first indicated that I wanted to go into law I was told by my family that it was not a profession for a woman. At that time, only two women had gone into law at McGill University, and only one of them finished the program and practised law. While the number of women in law at the University of Montreal was higher, the majority at that time were still men. Women had difficulty obtaining jobs in law firms. When they were hired, they were usually assigned to family law cases or relegated to handling cases considered to be of less importance than those assigned to men.

Although my experience with discrimination was limited, sexism was far more prevalent, particularly when I was working as a lawyer. In one health and safety case that I pleaded concerning a client's back injury, a medical specialist wondered out loud when I was cross-examining him what my back would look like if I had no clothes on. I immediately requested that the adjudicator ask the doctor to apologize, or I would not continue. The adjudicator supported me, and I obtained an apology. I also won my case.

On occasion, I received inappropriate remarks from my male colleagues. When I won my first case in court, a senior member of the firm asked me whether I had raised my robe and shown my lovely legs. I was especially angry knowing that a male lawyer would no doubt have been celebrated for his success. I firmly stated that I had handled the case well, had successfully represented a client of the firm, and had not lifted my robe. Another incident took place after a federal leader of a party had patted the bottom of a woman who was president of the party. While she responded in kind, the federal leader was painted by the media as being out of touch with women's issues. A senior member at my law firm patted my backside just as the federal leader had done. I was outraged and said so. Thankfully, I was not shy, and I demanded respect from my male colleagues.

Over the course of time, more and more women have entered law school, and the number of female lawyers has increased, as has the number of women judges. By the time I became a judge, it was not unusual to see a woman lawyer in the courtroom during trial. In fact, I learned that, one year, the number of women who were in law school at the University of Montreal exceeded the number of men. One day I could not help noticing that, in addition to the two women who usually accompanied me—namely, my assistant and my bailiff—both lawyers in the hearing and both of their clients were also women. In short, the staff and all the players in the courtroom were female. Since it had been a male-dominated profession for so long, it was most unusual for me to see that everyone present was a woman. I actually remarked on the fact in court.

During the time I sat on the Court of Quebec, a woman was appointed as the chief justice of the court, and, subsequently, another female judge headed this court. Before I retired, a woman was named chief justice of the Court of Appeal, and, in 2024, a woman still held this position. At the federal level, in 2019, the judiciary was slowly moving closer to gender parity. Since then, the proportion of all federally appointed judges who are women has increased and, as of December 2024, 47 percent of 1195 federally appointed judges were women. In the province of Quebec, according to statistics in 2024, women held 53 percent of the 326 judicial positions.[1] This is a far cry from the time when I was an undergraduate student and was told that law is not a career for a woman to consider.

The question may arise as to whether women act differently than men as judges. Many believe that women are more sensitive or more compassionate than men. I don't think so. There are many female judges who are caring and display empathy toward the parties in court, but there are also male judges who display the same behaviour. At the same time, I have observed female judges who are tough and strict and whose behaviour is indistinguishable from

---

Chapter 15

1 Information obtained from the judicial website in Quebec. "La Cour du Québec," *Cour du Quebec*, online: <courduquebec.ca/documentation-center/statisticscourduquebec.ca>.

what is often considered "male behaviour." In short, stereotypes do not actually exist.

Personally, I do not believe that the increase of female judges on the court has changed the dynamics of judging in any way. On the other hand, the increase of women on the bench better reflects their representation in our society and that, in itself, is a positive change.

THE FACE OF THE COURT

At the opening of the courts one year, in one of the speeches, the speaker stated that "the courts are too male, too pale, and too frail." This obviously was, and for the most part still is, the public image of our courts. When I was named to the bench, the majority of its judges were Caucasian men over the age of fifty. In the ensuing years, as already mentioned, more and more women have been named judges. As for age, it is evident that judges are not young. One must be a member of the bar for at least ten years before one can even apply to become a judge, and a position on the bench is considered the final stage of a legal career. Judges are virtually never named before the age of forty, and it is rare that judges are appointed under the age of forty-five.

There remains, however, the issue of race. Nearly all judges in Quebec are still Caucasian and francophone. When I was named to the Court of Quebec, there were only two Black judges. Since then, Juanita Westmoreland has retired, as has Daniel Dortelus, and only one other has been named to replace them. Those from ethnic, cultural, and visible minorities are few and far between. During my time at the court, other than my francophone colleagues, we had a couple of judges of Italian descent in the Civil Division. As for anglophones, there were two of us out of more than thirty judges in the Civil Division of the Court in Montreal. There were not many more in the entire province of Quebec, consisting of approximately three hundred judges.

Is it necessary to have representation from various groups in our society? Many would say yes, particularly in Montreal, which is a very cosmopolitan city and where approximately 40 percent of the population is not French speaking. There are many different ethnic groups in Montreal as well as in other Canadian cities. Litigants who present cases before a court that does not have any representatives from their community may well feel uncomfortable.

However, for the face of the court to change, pressure must be brought by the interested groups who seek representation on the bench as well as from the legal profession. Measures must be taken by the Bar Association, the courts, and, most importantly, the government to modify the composition of the bench and establish a more diverse court. Change is slow, but it remains possible.

Chapter 16

The Emotional Cost of Law

Civil lawsuits in the Court of Quebec are concerned with a claim for money and, for the most part, do not involve the emotional drama that takes place in family law cases. However, situations can occur not only in court but also outside the courtroom that impact on judges, who are expected to be serene at all times.

I experienced my share of emotional situations over the years—from the loss of my closest friend in law school, and, later, the loss of my cat, to suffering serious injuries as a result of accidents and having to live elsewhere than in my home during extensive renovations. As well, cases where we were asked to confine people affected with mental health issues to health institutions were challenging and, at times, upsetting to hear. Although it was rare, we heard cases on occasion that brought forth laughter and gave us some respite from the seriousness of a hearing. A number of these situations are described in this chapter.

STUDY SESSIONS

In law school, I became friends with Lorena Cavaliere, a woman who was not only blonde, pretty, and lively but also the brightest and most ambitious person in the class. She singled me out in the law library and asked me to study with her. Perhaps it was because I was the only other person in the library on the day classes began. We soon formed a study group.[1] We divided up our courses, with each group member being responsible for compiling a complete set of notes that contained virtually the exact contents of the professors' lectures. The notes were precious, and we guarded them jealously.

During our final year of law school, Lorena told us that she had been diagnosed with cancer. I drove her to and from the hospital every week for her chemotherapy treatments. She suffered all the typical symptoms related to the treatment but refused to end her studies. She wanted so very much to obtain her law degree so that her tombstone could read: "Maitre Cavaliere." I painfully recall one study session when we were reviewing our notes on successions, and Lorena asked us how people are buried in the winter when the ground is frozen solid. Lorena did not have to worry about a winter burial. She made it through the winter and wrote her exams, but she passed away in the spring of our last year of law school. She sat beside me in every class, helped me with my studies, and was one of my closest friends throughout our program. I was devastated by her passing.

While in law school, there was a television series called "Paper Chase" that I watched every week. Modeled on Harvard Law School, it portrayed a group of law students at an

---

1 We were a small group of women, which included Ava Kanner, another close friend. We met every weekend at Lorena's house where we enjoyed a delicious Italian meal that her mother cooked.

Ivy League university who studied together and succeeded because of their study group.

Each program ended with a song that talked about the initial years of law school being difficult, even more than anticipated. The song goes on to say that when this group of students is open to new ideas and is surrounded in their classes by good friends, who care about them, eventually these students will all be able to say that they have come through the first years.

Once Lorena passed away, I was unable to watch that television program or listen to that song. It reminded me too much of my study sessions with Lorena, and I truly missed our friendship.

OVERTURNED ON APPEAL

No judge wants to be told that a party, who considers that the judge is wrong, has appealed his decision or that the judgment he has rendered has been overturned on appeal. Unfortunately, this happens from time to time. While I considered including this section when I spoke about the possibility of judge's erring, I ultimately found that it was the emotional ramification of these appeals that I wanted to talk about.

Interestingly, judgments from the Court of Quebec are appealed less often than judgments from the Superior Court. This is not because judges at the Court of Quebec render better judgments but, rather, because the parties who have litigated in the Superior Court can directly appeal a judgment to the Court of Appeal if they wish to do so. Parties who are dissatisfied with a judgment of the Court of Quebec must first obtain permission from the

Court of Appeal before lodging an appeal, and permission is not given automatically.

To the best of my knowledge, only four of the several hundred judgments I wrote when I sat at the Court of Quebec were brought to the Court of Appeal. Each time this occurred, however, it was necessarily upsetting for me.

In one of the cases, a lawyer instituted a lawsuit against a client for his legal fees. I found that, in carrying out his mandate, the lawyer had charged an excessive amount of time for research, for the preparation of letters, discussions, and other matters. Multiple charges simply listed "exchange of e-mails," and many others were totally devoid of any details. The lawyer's *Code of Ethics* stipulates that fees must be fair and reasonable.[2] Our courts have declared that billing a client should not be a simple process of multiplying a lawyer's hourly rate by the number of hours spent on a file. Rather, lawyers must exercise their judgment as to the value of the services rendered and must carefully review the charges to determine the proper amount to be billed.

In the case I heard, I concluded that the amount of fees charged was not fair and reasonable, as required by the lawyer's *Code of Ethics*. As a result, I considerably reduced the amount of fees the lawyer sought. The lawyer requested permission to appeal my judgment. He claimed, among other reasons, that I had referred to several sections of the *Code of Ethics* that were not pertinent. In essence, he wanted the Court of Appeal to review the same evidence but come to a different conclusion. However, as the court pointed out in its judgment, this is not the role of the Court of Appeal. Moreover, the court stated that I had justified

---

Chapter 16

2 *Code of Professional Conduct of Lawyers*, CQLR c B-1, r 3.1, s 102.

my decision; it was based on the evidence at trial. The lawyer had not shown any manifest error that would allow the court to question my conclusions. His appeal was dismissed, and my judgment was maintained.

In a second case, where I had granted compensation to a dismissed employee, the employer obtained leave to appeal. In a very short judgment, the Court of Appeal stated that the employer wanted the court to redo the evaluation of the facts and replace my opinion with its own opinion. The court reiterated its position—namely, that it does not intervene to re-evaluate the evidence and change the judgment unless the appellant shows a manifest and determinant error in the trial judge's appreciation of the facts in the first instance. This was not the case in the judgment under appeal, and, consequently, the appeal was dismissed. This is most often the case as it was in the third instance where one of my judgments was appealed.

However, I had a surprise in a fourth case, which proceeded as follows. Mrs. P. instituted a lawsuit against Mrs. C., claiming that Mrs. C. had signed an acknowledgement of a debt in her favour. Mrs. C. admitted that she had signed the acknowledgement of the debt since she owed the money to Mrs. P., but she stated that she was bankrupt at the time. Given her situation, she claimed that she did not have the capacity to sign the acknowledgement.

The legalities of the case were complicated. Suffice it to say that it was clear that Mrs. P. could not sue Mrs. C. on the basis of a legal obligation. However, I considered that Mrs. C. had incurred a moral obligation to reimburse her debt, and this obligation had continued. I stated that the document that Mrs. C. had signed—known as a "reaffirmation agreement"—was valid and was not governed by the *Bankruptcy and Insolvency Act.*[3] I concluded that Mrs. C. was responsible for her undertaking and had to repay the debt that she had acknowledged. In support of the position I had adopted, I cited a reference to this type of agreement from a well-known text, *The Annotated Bankruptcy and Insolvency Act*. I also cited case law to substantiate my judgment.

The Court of Appeal did not agree. They accepted to hear the case and overturned my judgment. I was angry. Not simply because that court held that I was wrong but also because I had consulted and obtained the advice of one of the leading experts in bankruptcy law in Canada.[4] After explaining the facts of my case, I had requested his assistance. He provided me with guidance and pointed me to a couple of cases on the subject, which he considered would resolve my dilemma. I followed his advice and cited the cases he had suggested.

While the Court of Appeal was a higher court of law, I believed that the person I had consulted, who was an authority on bankruptcy law, was more knowledgeable on the subject than the judges on the Court of Appeal. However, I could not publicly say so. I therefore remained silent, but I was nevertheless angry with the outcome.

---

3 *Bankruptcy and Insolvency Act*, RSC 1985, c B-3.

4 It is not usual to seek advice outside of the judiciary or our legal department. However, I recall that when I was a lawyer, a Superior Court judge had called one of the partners at our law firm for advice on a labour law matter.

PSYCHIATRIC ASSESSMENTS AND CONFINEMENT IN A HEALTH INSTITUTION

One aspect of our jurisdiction is referred to as being *en chambre* or in chambers.[5] In such assignments, in addition to cases involving requests for a restricted licence and requests to have a seizure of a car lifted, we heard cases involving psychiatric assessments and confinements in a health institution. Although we referred to our hearings as being "in chambers," in reality, judges heard these cases in court. However, the psychiatric cases are not open to the public. These cases were incredibly taxing on our emotions.

Judges who sit in the Superior Court of Quebec have the authority to order medical treatment for individuals who require treatment but refuse it or are incapable of giving their consent. However, the same judges do not have jurisdiction to order a person's confinement in a health or social services institution. Judges who sit on the Court of Quebec, on the other hand, have the authority to order psychiatric evaluations and confinements in a health or social services institution, but they cannot order medical treatment. It is a dysfunctional system, but neither the Superior Court nor the Court of Quebec is willing to relinquish its jurisdiction. This means that when an individual who needs medical treatment in a hospital and does not have the capacity to give his consent or opposes being institutionalized, a lawyer seeking the necessary medical treatment for the individual in question must first obtain an order from the Court of Quebec to confine the concerned individual in an institution and then go to the Superior Court to obtain an order for treatment.

5 "In chambers" refers to a hearing that is held in a judge's office.

In order for a person to be placed under confinement in a health institution for a psychiatric assessment, judges at the Court of Quebec must have serious reasons to believe that, because of a person's mental health, that person is a danger to himself or to others. Following a psychiatric assessment, a judge can confine a person in an institution for a specific period of time. This requires that two psychiatrists consider that confinement is necessary and that the court itself has serious reasons to believe the person is dangerous and that confinement is necessary.

When we sat in chambers, we heard on average fifteen cases each morning; on occasion, we had many more. Our assignments in this area were set for one week at a time, and, generally, we dealt with these types of files only two or three weeks during the year. This is because the assignment was both demanding and emotionally draining. The uncontested cases of confinement were quick; the files were delivered complete with psychiatric evaluations. Representations were made by lawyers of the hospital involved in each file, and orders from the court were issued immediately when the evidence was clear.

The contested cases, on the other hand, were often filled with drama. In one instance, the hospital sought the confinement of a man who was suffering from a bipolar illness and had stopped taking his medication. He had been found walking naked along a popular street filled with boutiques and restaurants, distributing money to everyone he passed on his route. The person concerned claimed that he had been smoking a joint and needed to go for a walk to clear his head. He had been wearing a caftan. It was extremely warm out, and, when he took off his caftan, he forgot that he was not wearing anything underneath it. He claimed that he had forgotten because of the joint he had earlier. "When did you smoke the marijuana," I asked. He replied that it was three days earlier. Although this was long before the legalization of weed, and there was no expert at court to establish the length of time that a person could be affected after smoking a joint, I doubted that the effect of the weed lasted that length of time. In any event, distributing one's money to strangers constitutes a danger to an individual's well-being. Despite his claims that he was perfectly all right, I ordered his confinement.

The necessity of confinement was evident in many cases, such as the person who was found by the police walking down the middle of a highway claiming that he was God, the individual who testified that he heard voices giving him instructions to hurt other people, the young man who threatened his parents with a kitchen knife, and the man who smashed his television set because he claimed that the announcer was arguing with him.

However, there were other cases where the individual concerned appeared completely mentally well. It was only during questioning that their illness became apparent. One example concerned a woman who sounded very functional. She claimed to be well and wanted to leave the hospital where she was confined. I asked her where she planned to go, and she replied that she intended to live with her boyfriend, a bus driver. I pursued the line of questioning, asking her where the boyfriend lived. She had no idea where his residence was. Finally, when questioned as to when she had last seen him, it turned out to have been a couple of years prior to her confinement in the hospital. There had been no contact between them since. Clearly, there was a disconnect with reality.

Another example concerned an Inuit woman who was diagnosed as suffering from psychosis with delusional beliefs of a religious nature. At first, she appeared very coherent, and I wondered why she had been confined. I began to question her about her religious affiliation. She then began sobbing, explaining that she was a member of one of the lost tribes of Israel and had been expelled from her country. She opposed any confinement order because she needed to be free to return immediately to the holy land. After she had testified, it was clear that she had lost contact with reality and needed to be hospitalized.

THE LACK OF SERENITY

Judges are expected to be serene when sitting in court and give every case their full attention. Even when a judge's life in general is calm and harmonious overall, there are necessarily times when a judge's personal affairs impact his well-being. The reasons vary and can include marital problems, illness or the illness of someone in a judge's family, conflicts within a family or even conflicts with colleagues, or other matters. The issues impacting on a judge's serenity range from those affecting a judge physically to those having an emotional impact.

I was not immune to unanticipated problems. I had a cat who became ill and was sick for many months in the final year of his life. When it was time to put him down, I made the necessary arrangements with the veterinarian. My husband brought our pet to the vet since I was in court that day. I had planned to go there later that day at the end of the trial in time for the lethal injection to be administered. At lunch time, I was contacted by the veterinarian, who told me that I had to come to her establishment right away; my cat was suffering too much, and I could not wait until the end of the day.

I immediately drove to the vet's office and was present when my cat was put down. I was terribly upset as any pet owner would understand. I cried throughout the drive as I returned to the courthouse. Then, after drying my eyes and putting on a lot of make-up, I went back in to continue the hearing. I remember the day so well. Despite the fact that I was distraught over my loss, I had to face the lawyers and litigants in a serene manner. They could not be privy to my personal problem.

Another disruption of my serenity was caused by Ms. S., a secretary who shared the office with my assistant, Josette. Ms. S. had a number of issues, including the fact that she did not like light in the office. She not only dimmed the lights on her side of the room but also lowered all the blinds. It was not possible to work in such a dark environment. I raised the issue with my colleague, who was her superior, and finally managed to have the blinds raised sufficiently to let in enough light in order to work.

In addition to darkening the office, Ms. S. made a lot of noise as she worked. In typing judgments, she used an outdated machine that made a clacking sound and rattled all day long. She was unpleasant and created problems for Josette. The strained relationship between her and Josette created problems for me. Josette was unhappy and complained bitterly, with reason. My colleague suggested that Josette and I move to another office; I wanted my colleague and Ms. S. to be the ones to move. We failed to agree. The situation in the office became so contentious and intolerable that I finally consulted my coordinator and begged her to do something. Ultimately, my colleague and her secretary, Ms. S., moved to another office down the hall. My life at work returned to normal once the move had taken place.

A further disruption in my life was the renovation of the home that my husband and I purchased after we married. The renovations were to take place over the summer months when I was on holiday. However, typical of virtually every project of that kind, not only did the cost exceed the estimates we had been given, but the time frame for completing the work also exceeded the given date.

We had sold our previous house and had to vacate it, but we could not move into the newly purchased house since it was still being plastered and painted, and there was dust and dirt everywhere. We first booked into an apartment hotel, but when it was clear that the work would be ongoing for another few weeks, we moved into a friend's home. I survived the ordeal, but it was most inconvenient to be living out of a suitcase, without most of my possessions at hand. Luckily, since judges wear robes in court, I was not uncomfortable wearing the same outfit to work day after day! While my dislocation did not affect my work in court, I was unable to work when I was not in my office in the courthouse. As a result, during the renovations, I spent many more hours at the courthouse than I usually did.

The biggest disruption to my role as a judge stemmed not from events that could potentially affect me while I was in court but, rather, from two separate accidents that resulted in lengthy absences from work. One involved a car accident in which I was hit while walking across the street, and the other occurred while skiing. In the first accident, I broke one hip and fractured my back, and, in the second, I fractured the other hip. I found it excessively difficult to be relegated to my house for months, but I had little choice. I tried to use the downtime profitably. During one of my extended periods of absence, many years ago, I learned how to use a smart phone. During the second absence, I spent considerable time reading a huge volume entitled *Objections* since dealing with evidence was one of my weak areas. Although some workers might delight in not having to go to work, I was anxious to return to my job. I enjoyed my work and was happy when my convalescence was over.

THE STOLEN MOTORCYCLE

We rarely get to laugh during trials. In one memorable case, the person claiming a theft of a motorcycle, who I shall call Ms. B., was a big blonde woman with an outgoing personality. I still recall how much everyone in the courtroom laughed during a particular explanation she provided in her testimony.

Ms. B. filed a lawsuit against her insurance company following the theft of her motorcycle. The company refused to pay her, claiming she had made false declarations. Ms. B. had met Mr. G., a truck driver, on an internet dating site. They began seeing each other, and Mr. G. moved into Ms. B.'s lodgings as co-renters. Ms. B. was passionate about motorcycles and finally realized her dream when she bought a Harley Davidson with a loan. The finance agreement was in her name since Mr. G. was unable to obtain credit. She was also the one who obtained the insurance contract for the motorcycle, even though she did not have a licence to drive the vehicle and did not know how to drive it. The two travelled together to California on the trips Mr. G. made as a truck driver. During those trips, he showed her how the job was done since she wanted to become a truck driver. She was interested in the work because it was well paid.

Their relationship ended sometime later. Mr. G. contacted her and asked to have the motorcycle. She allowed him to have it provided that he paid the monthly payments as well as the cost of the insurance. However, Mr. G. failed to respect his agreement. As a result, Ms. B. went to his residence and took the motorcycle back.

Ms. B. developed a relationship with someone else. Sometime later, she and her new boyfriend were travelling on the motorcycle. He was driving the bike since she did not yet have her licence, and, on a highway, her boyfriend accidently dropped the key to the motorcycle. She went to the store where she had purchased the bike and told them that when she bought the bike she had only received one key, not a set of two. They told her that they did not have it. Ms. B. believed that her ex—namely Mr. G.—must have picked up the other key at some point. Shortly after that, Ms. B. decided to sell her motorcycle in order to buy a smaller and lighter one, which she thought she could bring with her in a truck when she became a truck driver. She advertised the bike but was unable to sell it.

One evening, she met her boyfriend at a restaurant for dinner. They had a fight and broke up. When she returned home, her motorcycle was gone. She reported the loss to the police and to her insurance company. According to the claims adjuster, there was a market in used parts, and there are many ways of stealing a motorcycle; he explained that a key is not necessary. Ms. B. suspected that her first boyfriend and former roommate, Mr. G., had stolen the bike using the key he had kept, but she had no proof.

The insurance company claimed that either there had not been a theft or, alternatively, that Ms. B. had participated in the disappearance of the bike. Among the principles that apply in such cases, the insurance company had to first establish that the participation of the insured in the theft was more probable than not. The insurance company presented circumstantial evidence. Among the facts it submitted, it contended that Ms. B. and Mr. G. were a couple, that the bike really belonged to Mr. G., and that Ms. B. needed to sell the bike for financial reasons. The insurance company also claimed that Ms. B. was hiding the identity of her then boyfriend, Mr. G. It pointed to the fact that Ms. B. had given the insurer a photograph but had cut out the image of the person sitting on the motorcycle.

Ms. B admitted that the insurance company wanted a picture of the motorcycle, but it had not asked for one showing someone sitting on the bike. She gave them a photograph where she had cut out the picture of Mr. G. on the bike. She explained that there was no reason to show who was on the motorcycle since the insurance company had only asked for a photo of the motorcycle. Moreover, she explained, she had removed the image of Mr. G. since he was completely naked. She had the original photograph with her of her ex, Mr. G., who was sitting on the motorcycle without any clothes on and offered it to the insurance company and to the court at trial. Needless to say, everyone was taken by surprise, and we all had a good laugh. At a tense time in the cross-examination of Ms. B., her offer to show Mr. G. in all his glory was welcome comic relief. As for the relationship of Ms. B. and Mr. G., Mr. G. stated that their relationship was one of co-renters "with privileges." We all found this not-so-subtle reference to their intimacy amusing.

The evidence showed that Ms. B. had purchased the motorcycle and was responsible for the payments. The evidence, however, failed to establish that Ms. B. was in financial difficulty and needed to sell the bike. Ms. B. eventually obtained her licence to drive a truck and got a job as a truck driver. Her next step was to get her licence to drive a motorcycle. I concluded that the proof that Ms. B. had made a false declaration was pure speculation. Good faith is presumed, and the insurance company had to prove bad faith on the part of the assured in order to succeed. The insurance company had not established, to my satisfaction, any fraudulent intention on the part of Ms. B. Consequently, I granted her claim.

Although I heard many lawsuits against insurance companies during my time on the bench, this case stands out because of the exuberant personality of Ms. B. and the emotional gaiety she provided during the trial.

Chapter 17

The Road to Mediation and Resolving Conflicts

Perhaps the person who was the most influential as a mentor for me in my career was Richard Hornung, who was a colleague of mine at the Canada Labour Relations Board. I must admit that I am remiss in never having confided this fact to him. Richard was smart, congenial, and had a great sense of humour. He was always very polite to the participants who appeared before the board, and he ran a very efficient hearing. An even greater asset was his capacity to mediate disputes, which he carried out in an informal manner.

I observed him on a number of occasions as he managed to settle difficult and contentious cases with ease. He would start talking to the parties and ask questions. It looked as if he came to the meeting of union and management representatives and decided on the spot how he would approach the discussions. I quickly learned that this was far from the case. He explained that his method was not haphazard; he had thought about the case and prepared for the mediation well before coming to the meeting. When I began mediating, after taking courses, I did my best to emulate his methods.

THE OLYMPIAN

I was sworn in as a judge on the Quebec Labour Court on a Friday, and, on the following Monday, I was assigned a case to hear, without having observed any other cases. This is not the usual situation for newly appointed judges. However, I knew that an observation period was not needed. I had already sat on numerous labour cases at the Canada Labour Relations Board. Although the Quebec Labour Code was not identical to the *Canada Labour Code*, and although the case law was different, most of the same type of issues were involved.[1] The principles in federal labour law and provincial labour law were essentially the same.

The case I was to hear on my first day on the bench in this court consisted of a complaint by a union member against his union for not representing him when he wished to file a grievance. I arrived at court and was faced with a number of procedures objecting to the testimony of an expert witness. The objection was based on the fact that he had not filed his expert report in conformity with the *Code of Civil Procedure*.[2] I had no interest in determining whether the objection was valid or not. More importantly, since I had virtually no experience practising civil law, I had no idea what was required under the *Code of Civil Procedure*. I was in a labour court, and I was not bound by the rules of a civil court.

I brought the parties into the conference room and asked them what the issue was and why a psychiatrist was present. I was told that the employee, who had filed the complaint, had asked for a leave of absence from his job

---

Chapter 17

1 *Canada Labour Code*, RSC 1985, c L-2.

2 *Code of Civil Procedure*, CQLR c C-25.

to train for the Olympics. Apparently, he did not participate in the games and later asked to have his job back. The union filed a grievance on his behalf and represented him. He then returned to work. The employee took a leave of absence a second time, and, again, he did not participate in the Olympics and asked to be reinstated in his job. He was successful this time as well. However, the third time that he left his job and then subsequently tried to return to work, his union refused to represent him—hence, his lawsuit.

And why the psychiatrist? Well, apparently, the employee had delusions that he could compete in the Olympics, but the reality was that he was not capable of competing; in fact, he was not a bona fide athlete. He had been under treatment for that very issue. The reason for the psychiatrist's presence was to confirm that the employee understood his limitations and that there was little risk that his past behaviour would be repeated.

After hearing the position of the employee and, particularly, the position of the psychiatrist, I began to discuss with the employer the possibility of the employee returning to work. Since the employee's performance had been very acceptable during the periods when he was at work, the employer readily agreed to reinstate him. Initially, the union representatives were opposed because the employee's return to work would impact on the seniority of the other employees in the bargaining unit. After I helped them work out the details of how the employee's seniority could be determined and how he could return to work without seriously affecting the seniority status of the other employees in his bargaining unit, the parties reached a deal. I handled the case with assurance and brought it to a successful conclusion.

This was very different from any judgment that I could render. My jurisdiction as a Labour Court judge was limited in such a case. If I had heard the case, I could reject the complaint or uphold it. If I upheld the complaint, all I could do was order that the case proceed to arbitration at the expense of the union. I could not have ordered the reinstatement of the employee. The agreement that the parties reached was truly a win-win situation since the employee got his job back and the union did not have to pay for another hearing that would have taken place before an arbitrator. After the settlement had been reached and the parties had left, my chief justice approached me and asked what had taken place since he had not seen me in the hearing room but had seen me going in and out of the conference room. I explained that I had been mediating the case. He asked what happened, and I proudly told him that the parties had reached a satisfactory agreement. He said: "But to conclude a case, there must be something in writing." I told him not to worry; I had a written agreement. He looked at me somewhat incredulously. "*Madame* Handman, how did you do that?"

As a result of that settlement, I established myself as the mediator of the court. Eventually, I handled all the mediation cases that arose.

THE WIN-WIN WAY

The aspect of my work that I enjoyed the most at the Court of Quebec was presiding over settlement conferences. We called such work "CRA," which stands for the French term "*Conference de règlement a l'amiable*." This, in essence, is a mediation in which a judge presides over the session. In such a proceeding, the judge, who is neutral and impartial, assists the parties involved in a lawsuit to reach a solution that is satisfactory to both parties.

However, when I was transferred to the Court of Quebec, settling cases was not the norm. When I talked about judges handling mediations, which I had done at the Labour Court, the reaction of my colleagues was hostile. I was told: "We are judges, not mediators," as if only judging was honourable and mediation was not.

One of the initial files that was assigned to me in this court involved an elderly man in his nineties. The parties asked for a postponement. I granted it provided that they agree to go to a settlement conference, despite the fact that such a process did not exist at the court at that time and despite the fact that imposing a condition was rather unconventional. The parties accepted my condition, and I met with them later that day.

The old man had instituted a lawsuit to annul a donation of the family's country home that he had made to one of his daughters. The daughter strongly contested the lawsuit. The father and his daughter had not talked to each other for a considerable period of time. What I first noticed was that the elderly man was extremely hard of hearing. His daughter, while not quite as deaf, also had a hearing problem. Having them sit on opposite sides of the table was not working. I asked them to sit beside each other and talk clearly and loudly into each other's ear. As the mediation progressed, they moved closer and closer to each other in order to better hear each other. They began to exchange information for the first time in many years.

It turned out that the idea of the donation came from the elderly man's wife who had since passed away. The elderly man had not approved the gift but went through with the donation to appease his wife. He subsequently decided that he wanted to repossess the house and spend time in the premises he had enjoyed throughout his life. However, his daughter and her husband had renovated the family country home and had no intention of losing what they had put into the property. His daughter wanted compensation for the renovations she had made in the house.

It was not long before the daughter was holding her father's arm while she was talking to him, and the solution became clear: the father would repay a portion of the renovations, and, as a counterpart, both he and his daughter, together with her husband, would share time at the country house. Before leaving the settlement conference, the father and daughter were hugging each other. I was afraid that my eyes would begin to tear because of their joyous embrace. It took every effort not to show my own emotions at this happy ending. A trial would never have produced such a positive result. I was subsequently congratulated for my initiative by the chief justice. I hoped that settlement conferences would become more accepted at the court.

I was right, but it took time for settlement conferences to be accepted by judges, lawyers, and the Bar Association. The culture has changed over the years but very slowly. Now, our courts encourage parties to attend settlement conferences, and lawyers have finally adopted this method as a means of dealing with lawsuits. While all provinces in Canada have some form of mediation procedures, Quebec is one of the very few locations where judges act as the neutral intermediary and try to help the parties to a dispute reach an agreement. In most other jurisdictions, the courts either order or recommend mediations, but the mediation sessions are carried out by certified mediators in the private sector.

TEACHING MEDIATION

Since I had instituted mediation procedures at the Quebec Labour Court and had experience teaching mediation techniques and lecturing on the subject to judges, lawyers, and mediators at various conferences in Montreal and Europe, it seemed to me that I could teach my mediation skills to my colleagues. I asked if I could participate in teaching the judges at the Court of Quebec in the mediation course that would be offered. I was told that I had to take the course before I could teach it.

I was frustrated and felt thwarted in my attempt to establish myself as an expert in the field, but I had no choice but to accept the court's rules. Interestingly, when I attended the training program, I was able to demonstrate a new step in the mediation procedure. It was one that I personally used since it was beneficial to the process. I intervened to such an extent that my colleagues asked the trainers to allow me to give a demonstration. I felt vindicated.

Sometime later, when I asked to teach the advanced mediation course given at the Court of Quebec and the course at the National Judicial Institute, I met the same resistance as I had when I first asked to participate in the training of judges. I never did understand why I was not given the opportunity to teach mediation at these sessions, particularly since I had trained judges at many international conferences in Europe, and I had also trained visiting judges at conferences held in Montreal.

My disappointment was tempered by the numerous letters of congratulations that I received over the years for my services as a mediator from the chief justice of the Court of Quebec, the associate chief justice, as well as from senior lawyers from various law firms. I appreciated the recognition I received from colleagues who, on several occasions, asked me if I would step in to mediate a difficult file that had been assigned to them. I also take comfort from the heartfelt thanks of many of the participants in my mediations as well as the people who I have trained both in Canada and in Europe.

While I have taught many mediation courses for over twenty-five years, given presentations, and written a book on the subject, I believe that mediating, to a large degree, is a natural skill. Intuition, empathy, and the ability to read and comprehend body language all come into play. I truly believe that mediation is a better way of handling litigation than proceeding before a judge in a trial. The parties have a chance to vent their emotions, and often the real cause of the conflict is discovered. This is not always the case in a trial. In mediation, each party walks away either totally satisfied or, at the very least, with some degree of satisfaction. This is more than can be said about the outcome of a lawsuit after a trial. In virtually all the cases in which the parties have agreed to the mediation process, they settle their dispute and respect their agreement. As the saying goes, "if there is a will, there is a way."

The following are some of my more memorable mediation cases.

PROBLEMATIC LAWYERS

Lawyers may be very helpful in assisting their clients to reach a settlement. On the other hand, lawyers on occasion pose obstacles to any possibility of a settlement. In one such case, an accountant who had lost his job had sued the company where he had been employed for over thirty-five years. He had worked for the owner, who was the head of the company, but that person had passed away, and the son had taken over the business. The parties had come to the mediation with their lawyers, but rather than assisting their clients to reach some sort of compromise, both lawyers were very contentious. There appeared to be no possibility of reaching any kind of agreement.

I said that I would like a coffee, and one of the lawyers offered to get one for me. I accepted but asked the other lawyer if he minded going with the opposing lawyer. When both were gone, I turned to the son, who was running the business, and asked him about the accountant's work. I also asked for more details about the company's decision to end his employment. According to the son, the accountant had not done anything wrong; it was simply that they were re-organizing, and his services were no longer needed.

I pointed out that he had offered virtually nothing in the way of compensation to an employee who had been with the company throughout his entire career. I then asked him what his father would have done had he been alive. The son at first appeared uncomfortable. Then he reacted as I had hoped he would. He suggested a monetary package that he thought his father would have offered. He and the accountant began to discuss the package and possible options. It was not long before they reached an agreement regarding an amount that was satisfactory not only for the accountant but for the company as well.

The two lawyers returned with my cup of coffee. As they entered the mediation room, they found the accountant and the son shaking hands on the deal they had reached. The lawyers looked startled and demanded to know what had happened. I replied that their clients had resolved their conflict and were satisfied.

I presided over this mediation case early on in my career at the Court of Quebec. I would do it differently now. I would ask the lawyers for their permission to talk to their clients on my own. In retrospect, what I had done was somewhat unorthodox. But, at the time, I was so frustrated with the obstacles that the lawyers had imposed, making it impossible to settle the case, that I simply wanted them to leave so that I could talk to their respective clients without the lawyers' interference. I was convinced that, without them, a deal could be reached. I was right. However, since lawyers are the representatives of the parties, and although I often preferred to meet with the parties on my own, it is clear that lawyers must agree that I can continue discussions with their clients in their absence.

AN INNOVATIVE SOLUTION

One mediation file with an unusual ending began as a typical case of hidden defects in a newly purchased house. The parties each presented their version of the facts. The seller understood and accepted that she was responsible for the problems the buyer had encountered following the purchase. She indicated that she would be willing to pay for the damages but that she only had a portion of the money needed for a settlement to take place and could not afford to pay the balance.

I had questioned the participants at the mediation session about their respective professions or occupations and learned that the seller (the woman who was sued) was a hairdresser. I asked if she would consider offering her hairdressing services as part of her payment. She readily agreed. I then turned to the purchaser, who had instituted the action, and asked if he would accept her offer, which was something that would benefit his wife. The purchaser looked at me as if I was mad and said that his wife would never agree. I simply suggested that we take a break and asked him to contact his wife.

He returned to the mediation session a short time later, looking somewhat sheepish. His wife was more than willing to have regular hairdressing services, including haircuts, styling, and hair dyes. The only questions that remained were the number of such services that would be available and over what period of time. These details were easy to work out. The parties settled their case by means of the seller making a partial payment, together with the provision of hairdressing services. This outcome served as the basis for me to encourage lawyers and parties to think "outside the box" and think of creative solutions to settle a conflict.

THE PARTY LINE

At the time I sat as a judge, mediating by means of videoconferencing was considered an innovative way of carrying out the process. I tried it in one of my cases not because I wanted to but, rather, because there was no other way to do the mediation. The employers were in Montreal; the couple who instituted the lawsuit had lived in Montreal but had left to live in Germany. Rather than have them return to Canada for either the trial or for a mediation session, we attempted to see if their conflict could be resolved by using what was then modern technology.

I must admit that I found it difficult. In addition to scheduling the session and taking into consideration the time difference between the two countries, there was the issue of eye contact, which did not always work very well. As well, there was the problem of having everyone interact with each other in a coherent manner. When one party is talking, he often does not hear that the other party had intervened until he has stopped talking.

Although the dynamics of the process were in themselves difficult, what made the case more complex was that, while the parties were talking with each other, we hit a party line and were intercepted by two people who intervened in the conversation. They were from South America, which in itself was rather strange, but even stranger was the fact that they happened to understand German. They had been able to follow the discussions that were taking place between the couple, although the whole process was confidential. I suggested that we hang up and try to connect again so that we could continue the discussions without our unwanted friends. We managed to do so, and the parties involved in my case eventually came to a solution.

At the time, I considered that having the parties separated and unable to speak directly to each other was not the most efficient way of handling such cases, and I preferred mediating with the parties present in person. That has since changed. Mediation by means of Zoom, Teams, or other platforms has become commonplace. It is quite convenient to proceed in this way. It eliminates travel time and is extremely efficient. As well, litigants often feel more comfortable participating in the process in the comfort of their own home or office.

THE ANGRY FATHER

Another difficult case involved a man ("the father") who felt that fathers were getting the short end of the stick when it came to divorce cases. He was furious with a particular newspaper that he considered had dealt with him and his position unjustly. He filed a lawsuit against the newspaper alleging defamation. Despite his anger, he agreed to come to mediation.

During the mediation session, he hurled insults at the opposing party and was verbally abusive. At one point, the representatives from the newspaper got up and told me they were leaving. They were not interested in hearing any more noxious language. There appeared to be no possibility of continuing the mediation session. I begged them to stay for just another five minutes and asked the father to follow me to another room where we could talk privately. When we were alone, I wanted to say that his behaviour was offensive, and it was totally understandable that the members of the opposite party were prepared to leave. Instead, I simply mentioned that a person gets more with honey than with vinegar.

The father looked at me in surprise, expecting a scolding and said: "What do you want me to do, apologize?" I replied: "You're an adult. I'm not going to tell you what to do. Do you want them to stay? If you want them to remain at the mediation session, I'm sure you know what to do." Without saying anything to me, the father returned to the room in which the mediation was taking place, apologized to the various representatives of the newspaper and asked them to stay.

Although this was one of the few cases that did not end in a settlement at the end of the mediation session, the outcome was not entirely dismal. The concerned father badmouthed the entire judicial system but stated that, for him, there were two exceptions: one concerned another judge and the other was me. He had not settled his case but was nevertheless satisfied with the process and with the fact that I had dealt with him fairly. He had also had the opportunity of expressing his dissatisfaction with the way in which the newspaper had handled his case and the impact it had had on him. In this particular case, his mediation experience, which for him was satisfactory, was sufficient for me.

MEDIATION TODAY

Since I retired, I have continued to preside over mediation sessions, speak at international conferences, and have even written a book on the topic.[3] I still strongly believe this process is very beneficial for parties who are involved in a dispute or a lawsuit. It provides a faster, less stressful, and less expensive means to deal with litigation, and it facilitates access to justice. Most importantly, mediation provides the parties with the possibility of determining the outcome of their litigation and even finding solutions that a court cannot order.

The subject is now taught in law schools and in continuing legal education courses for lawyers and has become part of the legal landscape. A significant change in dealing with conflict has occurred since the time I first advocated mediation in the Court of Quebec and was told that we were judges, not mediators.

3 Suzanne Handman, *Mediation for Lawyers: A Practical Guide for Effective Representation of Your Clients* (Toronto: Irwin Law, 2024).

Chapter 18

The End of a Career

Retirement is not easy for most judges, who are used to the ongoing stimulation of the work involved and the relationships that they build during their time on the bench. The administration of the court tries to prepare judges for their retirement by offering courses and advice beforehand. There is also a retirement party given to the judge who is leaving. Some judges elect to continue as supplementary judges, while others leave to enjoy their leisure time. The end is bittersweet. There is more time to participate in activities that were not available before and more time to travel and spend with family and friends. At the same time, there is also a sense of loss—that is, the loss of no longer being *Monsieur le juge* or *Madame le juge*, with all the trappings that go along with the title.

While it took some time to adjust, I eventually became involved in several different activities, both those connected to my profession and those that simply give me pleasure, as is the case of most other retired judges.

GETTING READY FOR RETIREMENT

The Court of Quebec offers a seminar for judges approaching their retirement, and I was eligible to attend the seminar a few years in advance of my retirement. It took place at a charming inn situated outside of Quebec City, and we were encouraged to bring our spouses with us. This was far more relaxed than other conferences I had attended, and having my husband join me was most enjoyable.

At the conference, we were given a binder containing a list of reminders regarding matters to be dealt with before our retirement, such as informing the court when we planned to retire, making decisions regarding our insurance plans, and filling out various forms. During the conference, experts spoke on various subjects, many of which were interesting, while others led to some confusion. The lectures dealt with our retirement regime, the calculation of our pension, financial planning, insurance options, and legal issues concerning subjects such as wills and a mandate in the event of incapacity. They also dealt with our health and factors that would impact on our well-being in the years to come as well as our psycho-social adaptation involving a loss in contacts, a decrease in activities, and a decrease in revenue.

The lectures on psycho-social adaptation were the most confusing. One psychiatrist strongly recommended that we make plans beforehand for what we would do once we retired so that we would be well prepared, while another specialist advised us to wait before making any plans and suggested that we retire first and then decide what we would like to do. There was a great deal of discussion amongst us about our future plans. Most of the men planned to continue as *juges suppléants* (supplementary judges) who work on an on-call basis and can continue to do so until the age of seventy-five. The female judges, on the other hand, looked forward to more leisure time in order to participate in activities that interested them, which included music lessons, cooking classes, travel, and so on.

When it was my turn to talk about the future, I was unable to speak about any plans. At that point, I was not ready to retire. I still had no Plan B to cover my life after I left the court. I was seriously concerned about what I would do. I did not want to be a supplementary judge or return to the practice of law as counsel, as some judges did, but, nevertheless, I wanted to continue working. The only possibility that came to mind was to begin a private mediation practice. However, I had not looked into how I would begin such an endeavour and had not made any concrete plans.

At the Court of Quebec, judges are required to retire from the bench when they reach the age of seventy (while, at the Superior Court, the obligatory retirement age is seventy-five). Years ago, that was considered to be very old. No one expected anyone to be sufficiently fit mentally to function well or to continue to work. However, given that life expectancy has increased so much, most judges who reach this number do not feel old or incapacitated in any way.

As already indicated, at the Court of Quebec, those who retire and choose to continue to work can do so as supplementary judges with no definite or regular schedule. The majority of cases that were assigned to retired judges at the Court of Quebec consisted of small claims cases. I was only interested in presiding over mediation cases, but this was not an available option. As a result, I left the court on my scheduled retirement date, with no plans to continue as a supplementary judge or any other plans for that matter. It took time after I left the bench to adapt to my new role, but, eventually, I did discover many satisfying activities that fill my life.

THE SPEECH

The Court of Quebec had an annual end of year party and used this occasion to provide a farewell to any judge who was retiring that year. I was told before the event that I and another judge would be feted at this party, and our husbands were invited to join us. As we drove to the party, I turned to my husband and asked if he thought I would be expected to give a speech. Having never attended such a party, he had no idea, but he suggested that I be prepared to say something if the occasion arose. I had not given any thought beforehand to giving a speech, and I prefer having my ideas on paper as opposed to giving a spontaneous presentation. As we were approaching the party area, I took out a small piece of paper and a pen I had in my purse and jotted down some thoughts.

Thank goodness I had done so. At the end of an elaborate meal with plenty to drink, I was toasted by a colleague and friend, David Cameron, in a most complimentary way and then I was asked if I wanted to say anything. My headings and the brief notes I had written on the way to the event were a godsend. I elaborated on my educational and work background, which many of my colleagues were unaware of, and talked about the difficulty I had when I first came to the Court of Quebec, pointing to my lack of knowledge of civil law. When I began, I only knew of a seizure as a medical term and not the legal term of forcibly taking possession of a person's property by legal means! Another example that I gave was the fact that for me, when numbers were raised at trial, it sounded like a highway outside of Quebec rather than various articles of the *Civil Code*. These examples, while true, made my colleagues laugh.

I thanked those who had been so helpful to me when I needed assistance and ended my remarks by looking forward to the future. Since I had not written out my speech beforehand and had not thoroughly thought about what I would say, I failed to mention, in describing how I saw my future, that I looked forward to spending more time with the most important person in my life—namely, my husband Bjørn.

MISSING ROYALTY STATUS

I ultimately did retire. I am no longer "Madam Justice" or the French version, "*Madame le juge*," or even "Your majesty" or "Your royal highness." Judges in the Superior Court of Quebec keep their title on retirement. In the Court of Quebec, that is not the case. We cannot use the title of My Lady or Madam Justice upon retirement. On the other hand, we can still use the title of "Judge." However, I virtually never do.

I miss being "royalty." In essence, that is how judges are treated in the legal world. Judges are recognized by all the players in the courthouse—from the lawyers, the clerks, and the bailiffs to the constables and those serving in the cafeteria—and are treated with the utmost respect and deference.

At first, after working 24/7, I welcomed my new freedom. I was able to sleep in; I had time to read the daily newspapers thoroughly and watch several Netflix series. I binged on one series, cramming several years into a short period. I became part of a film group, which met every Monday evening to watch a movie and then go out to dinner. I could not do that when I sat since I could never leave work early enough to attend an early film and then join friends at a restaurant.

Other perks included being able to travel when I wanted to. Although I did travel extensively while I was a judge, I now had even more time and did not have to wait until set periods, such as summertime, when it was generally high season. I went with my husband to New York and then to Europe in the first few months of retirement and, subsequently, to many other destinations. I attended mediation conferences in Europe without being concerned that it reduced my vacation time. There was also more time to host dinner parties, meet friends, and shop.

I was no longer subjected to the *obligation de reserve*—namely, the obligation of not speaking publicly about any issue that could impact upon the image of the court. I could express any opinion I had, even if it was politically incorrect. "Life was good"—for a while. The novelty of my free time soon wore off. When I was asked what I did (for a living), I said I had just retired. The response was invariably: "Congratulations." My bitter reply was: "Why are you congratulating me. ... I had to leave because I became old." That obviously resulted in silence on the part of my interlocutor.

I missed the status of my position. But what I missed just as much was an activity that allowed me to feel that I was still contributing to society in a positive way. I began to seek other means of both connecting with my profession and remaining useful to society. One of the activities that I enjoyed immensely while I was working as a judge was mediating disputes. In fact, I was convinced that this type of alternate dispute resolution mechanism was far more effective in resolving disputes than litigation before the courts. I wanted to continue mediating and took steps to do so.

After retirement, I presided over mediation sessions at the courthouse and now continue to preside over mediations in private practice. I find this work very rewarding. It gives me great pleasure to help parties reach a satisfactory agreement after a legal conflict has arisen. I have given presentations on mediation at international mediation conferences in Europe as well as lectures to lawyers at various organizations in Montreal. I have been asked to present a conference on mediation to mediators by the Montreal Bar Association and have agreed to do so. These are volunteer activities, but I have gladly accepted them and still accept the requests I receive. It gives me the sense of purpose that I needed.

A connection to my profession remained important to me, and so I continue to be involved in legal affairs. I became involved in an organization called Justice de Proximité de Grand Montréal, a non-profit group that provides legal information to the public. I was asked to join the Board of Directors of this organization, and I was also asked if I would give lectures to the public on how to present a claim or a defence before the Small Claims Court of the Court of Québec. I accepted both the board position and lecturing and exercised these functions on a regular basis for several years.

Other activities include my attendance at the events of the Lord Reading Law Society. I act as a mentor under a Montreal Bar Association program for young lawyers and have mentored and continue to mentor young lawyers who seek advice about changing their career orientation or about issues involving work/life balance. Several mentees have kept in contact with me, even after having successfully changed their employer. Mentoring has been a very meaningful experience. The ongoing relationships that I have with these young lawyers are a source of satisfaction for me.

I should add the role of grandmother to my list of activities. I am constantly amazed at the time, effort, and particularly the patience that are required to keep young kids engaged and interested in any pursuit. I adore my grandchildren but must admit that I am not the perfect grandmother—namely, the one who jumps in to take care of the children all day long on a regular basis.

I have finally adapted to my new identity—that of a retired but active woman. My leisure activities also include participation in a book club and oil painting courses. I discovered that some of my mother's artistic talent has apparently been passed on to me. I paint regularly, and this is one of the activities that I enjoy the most. I have made new friends in my courses and have added over a dozen pieces of my own artwork to our already overcrowded walls. I also have exhibited my artwork at a few group exhibitions. I began to study Norwegian, a most difficult task, so that I could talk to my husband's family and friends in their own language. I am not yet fluent but am very proud to be able to carry on a conversation in this Nordic language. And, during the pandemic, I wrote a text on mediation for lawyers, which was published in 2024.

I remain a type "A" with a need to excel and achieve. I have other projects in mind that I wish to achieve in the future. Hopefully, they will materialize.

NEW REALITIES

COVID-19 broke out in the winter of 2020. Our way of life was changed, and the courts were not spared. As a result of social distancing, the courts closed for all matters except urgent cases, such as restraining orders, family matters that had to be resolved quickly, and requests for confinement of individuals who presented a danger to themselves or to others. The courts functioned by means of Microsoft Teams for a few months, and obligatory continuing legal education for lawyers took place online. Professional conferences and meetings also took place by Microsoft Teams or Zoom. For judges, the absence of a regular schedule of hearing cases necessarily meant that they could catch up on their backlog of judgments, which was a rare opportunity.

However, while the courts finally re-opened, a number of legal activities have changed, perhaps forever. Some changes began before the pandemic. At the main courthouse, everyone outside the legal profession entering the building must pass through security. Judges and staff carry identification cards that allow them entrance to the judges' chambers, whereas before a key was sufficient.

Since my retirement, mediating in consumer cases as well as most of the small claims cases that are mediated now take place online. Court proceedings can now be filed online, and more and more judges use their computers in the courtroom for taking notes during a trial, reviewing exhibits filed in evidence, and even verifying provisions in their codes and reading case law. The use of Teams, which was used only in exceptional cases when a party could not be present at court, has become far more prevalent.

Law as a profession is slow to change. Consider the fact that lawyers and judges in Quebec still wear black robes and white bibs, as they did centuries ago. Despite the modifications to our *Civil Code* and *Code of Civil Procedure* to facilitate proceedings, there are still often multiple proceedings filed in cases, litigation is extremely costly, and the time it takes for a case to come to trial is far too long. However, in other aspects, the practice of law has changed considerably since I was a young lawyer. It is inconceivable today to imagine drafting proceedings by hand. It is also inconceivable to imagine researching manually by taking volumes of books off the library shelf one at a time and reading hard copies of judgments as I did many years ago. Although I have adapted to many of the technological changes that have taken place over the past few years, I am nevertheless happy that my retirement came at the time it did.

MY TIME ON THE BENCH

As I said at the outset, when I was named a judge, I felt as if I had won the lottery. I still feel that way. My career on the bench was fascinating. I learned so much not only about different areas of the law but also about so many aspects of everyday living, ranging from service contracts and construction contracts to medical liability and how banks function. There were never two days that were identical, and I was never bored.

Prior to applying to become a judge, I had undergone some psychological testing for career choices. What I found to be most interesting were the results of the tests I had taken, which indicated that I would thrive as a marketing representative, sales representative, or trainer. I was classified as an extrovert with skills in public speaking and persuasion. I was counselled never to consider one particular field as a career—that of a position as a judge since it was seen to be solitary work and did not correspond to my personality.

However, I enjoyed reading the case law in any given area of the law. Contrary to some of my colleagues, who liked deciding a case but hated writing their decisions, I actually enjoyed sitting by myself and drafting judgments. A blank page never frightened me, and I enjoyed working alone. I worked hard. Except for the time that I was away on holiday and out of the country, I never ceased thinking about my cases and the judgments that I had to write. My cases permeated my thoughts at virtually all times when I was not in the courtroom, whether I was in my office drafting or whether I was taking a break and walking to the store around the corner. When I awoke at night, I often thought about how I would resolve a case. I know that this is not unusual, although most people in the profession will not admit to such a preoccupation. However, a few lawyers I am friendly with have acknowledged that they think about their cases all the time, and it is only when they are out of town that they are able not to think about them. Judges necessarily have the same tendency.

One of my paramount considerations while I was working was doing what was right. That meant not only rendering a decision that had accurately related the facts and was correct in law but, to the extent possible, rendering a decision that was just. In most cases, even when I looked for a conclusion that was fair, the outcome dictated by the law was the conclusion that I had already reached. In a very small number of cases, when the law appeared to be unjust, I sought to find an equitable solution.

I would not be honest if I did not admit that I enjoyed the status that came with being a judge. I liked the recognition that I was granted not only by all the court staff but also by other professionals and the public. I often witnessed a change in attitude when people learned that I was a judge. In many cases, I noted that, when dealing with older professional men who were not used to women in so-called men's professions, I went from being a client, a patient, or someone's wife to a person who had standing in their eyes. As I have already said, I miss being Madam Justice or "Madame le Juge." But I had the privilege of working under that title, and I am forever grateful.

Index

ABOUT THE AUTHOR

Suzanne Handman obtained a law degree from the University of Montreal, after an initial career as a clinician and Associate Professor in Speech Therapy and Audiology. She joined the firm of Trudel, Nadeau and associates, which specialized in labour law, and subsequently became a partner.

In 1994, she was appointed a Vice Chair of the Canada Labour Relations Board (now the Canada Industrial Relations Board) and in 2000, she was appointed Judge of the Quebec Labour Tribunal. In 2005, she transferred to the Civil Division of the Court of Quebec.

During her career on the Bench, Judge Handman began a mediation program at the Quebec Labour Tribunal. At the Court of Quebec, in addition to presiding over trials, she was very active conducting settlement conferences.

Now retired, Suzanne Handman continues to mediate conflicts. She is on the Board of Directors of the International Mediation Council, has given presentations at conferences in Montreal and in Europe, and has authored several articles and a book on mediation. She also regularly mentors young lawyers. Her other activities include an active participation in a book club and learning Norwegian. She is passionate about painting and has exhibited in several group exhibitions.

Suzanne Handman is married to Bjørn U. Ellingsen and lives in Montreal.